I0801847

Interdisciplinary Research in Mathematics, Science, and Technology Education

Committee on Research in Mathematics, Science,
and Technology Education
Commission on Behavioral and Social Sciences and Education
National Research Council

NATIONAL ACADEMY PRESS
Washington, D.C. 1987

COMMITTEE ON RESEARCH IN MATHEMATICS, SCIENCE, AND TECHNOLOGY EDUCATION

1984-1986

JAMES G. MARCH (Chair), Stanford University (political science)
ARNOLD B. ARONS, University of Washington (physics)
W.O. BAKER, Bell Telephone Laboratories, Inc., retired (chemistry)
MICHAEL COLE, University of California, San Diego (psychology)
MARGARET B. DAVIS, University of Minnesota (biology)
FREDERICK ERICKSON, University of Pennsylvania (anthropology)
ROBERT GLASER, University of Pittsburgh (education, psychology)
ANDREW M. GLEASON, Harvard University (mathematics)
MICHAEL A. GUILLEN, Harvard University (mathematical physics)
JILL H. LARKIN, Carnegie-Mellon University (psychology and educational computing)
CORA B. MARRETT, University of Wisconsin (sociology)
SAMUEL J. MESSICK, Educational Testing Service, Inc., Princeton, N.J. (psychometrics)
PAUL E. PETERSON, Brookings Institution, Washington, D.C. (political science)
MARE TAAGERERA, University of California, Irvine (chemistry)
DAVID E. WILEY, Northwestern University (education)

SENTA A. RAIZEN, Study Director
ROLF K. BLANK, Research Associate

Preface

The Committee on Research in Mathematics, Science, and Technology Education was established by the National Research Council in 1984 to help improve education in these fields through research and the application of research results. Subsequently, the National Science Foundation asked the committee to prepare this report because of its interest in fostering involvement of scientists in collaborative research with educators to address problems in science and mathematics education.

Over the past several years, there have been examples of successful collaboration among mathematicians and natural scientists who are concerned with the structure and development of knowledge in their fields, behavioral and social scientists who are concerned with how students learn, and educators with experience in the classroom. While these collaborations have proved productive for mathematics and science education, there has been a paucity of this kind of work, in part because the organization of research along disciplinary lines and current academic incentive systems do not encourage scientists to engage in interdisciplinary research, particularly in an applied area like education. A forthcoming report by the Committee on Basic Research in the Behavioral and Social Sciences (1987) makes the point more generally: promising opportunities for interdisciplinary collaboration exist in many basic and applied research fields but will demand creative innovations in modes of research-support and operation of academic institutions.

In this report the committee attempts to answer several practical questions with regard to increasing interdisciplinary research in science and mathematics education: What kinds of problems in science and mathematics education need an interdisciplinary research approach? What can be learned about incentives and strategies for interdisciplinary research from previous interdisciplinary projects in science and mathematics education and from interdisciplinary research in other fields? What specific programatic initiatives by a federal agency are likely to increase the interest and activity of scientists, education researchers, and educators in interdisciplinary research?

This is the second report of the committee. In its initial report, Mathematics, Science, and Technology Education: A Research Agenda (1985), the committee recommended directions for research that would address critical problems in the teaching and learning of science and mathematics in schools: developing student skills in reasoning and problem-solving, improving the quality of the curriculum and teaching in science and mathematics, restructuring the classroom to allow for more hands-on learning experiences, and applying information technology to mathematics and science education. Many of the research priorities identified in the committee's first report in fact call for interdisciplinary work of the kind discussed in this report.

The committee is grateful to many people for their assistance in preparing this report. The scientists and mathematicians who were leaders of the curiculum projects in the 1960s made a major contribution by providing us with information and insight from their experience. We also want to thank the National Science Foundation for support of the committee for this project; special appreciation is extended to Raymond Hannapel of the Foundation's Science and Engineering Education Directorate, who encouraged the committee to pursue a study on this topic. Appreciation is due also to the National Research Council staff, who made our work possible. Senta Raizen, study director, made major contributions to the substance and organization of this report, as did Rolf Blank, research associate. Eugenia Grohman, associate director for reports of the Commission on Behavioral and Social Sciences and Education, added to the clarity of the report and managed its production.

JAMES G. MARCH, Chair
Committee on Research in
Mathematics, Science, and
Technology Education

Contents

1
The Role of Interdisciplinary Research

THE NEED FOR CHANGE

This report makes two arguments: that interdisciplinary research is important for the improvement of mathematics, science, and technology education and that good interdisciplinary research is possible. Although it is probably easier to secure agreement on the first argument than on the second, neither is self-evident.

In an earlier report (Committee on Research in Mathematics, Science, and Technology Education [hereafter, Committee], 1985), this committee discussed the importance of bringing together different disciplines and different perspectives in improving mathematics, science, and technology education. The present report summarizes that discussion, gives specific examples of the need for collaborative research, explains why such collaboration is difficult to sustain, and provides some procedures for furthering it.

The need to improve the quality of teaching and learning in mathematics, science, and technology education in the United States has been well documented (National Science Board Commission on Precollege Education in Mathematics, Science and Technology Education, 1983; National Assessment of Educational Progress, 1983a, 1983b; Hueftle et al., 1983; Task Force on Education for Economic Growth, 1983; Crosswhite et al., 1985; Jacobson and Doran, 1985; McKnight et al., 1987). These studies show that effective education in those fields is impeded by minimal high school graduation requirements, the rote learning orientation of science curricula, the bureaucratic structure of educational institutions, and the limited incentives for recruitment and retention of well-qualified teachers. The catalogue of deficiencies is easy to produce. Correcting them is not.

As we noted previously (Committee, 1985:1-2), the deficiencies in mathematics, science, and technology education are not primarily the result of ignorance or incompetence, but, rather, of choices made by American society in allocating personal and collective resources and effort. Those choices include the obvious ones of the aggregate levels of resources devoted to mathematics, science, and technology education and to research to improve that education. They also include the less obvious choices reflected in the innumerable responsibilities and constraints imposed on schools by parents, professional associations, communities, and public authorities. And they include the choices of American parents in allocating personal resources of time and money to supplementing, encouraging, and supporting the educational efforts of schools, as well as in providing extracurricular and recreational activities for children.

As citizens, the members of the present committee think some of these choices unwise and inefficient. However, our assignment here is not to campaign for political or social support for mathematics, science, and technology education. Rather, our charge is to suggest ways of improving that education within the broad choices reflected in society. We believe that significant improvements can be achieved within the framework of contemporary American society. Educational institutions change frequently enough to lend credence to the possibility of managing that change to some degree.

"Managing change to some degree," however, is different from adopting policies or promulgating edicts. The surface credibility of introducing educational change through simple fiat (e.g., governmental policy, pronouncements, or legislation) conceals some major complexities. First, changing education may require changes in many different, interrelated institutions, including universities, publishing companies, professional associations, labor unions, employers' organizations, courts, public agencies, and families, as well as schools. Each of these institutions is itself a complicated collection of cooperating and competing groups and individuals.

Second, the scientific base for beneficial change is fragmented and incomplete. In our previous report, the committee stressed the importance of research aimed at increasing the amount and quality of active, fruitful learning time for students of mathematics, science, and technology. Cognitive studies of learning are providing more understanding of the nature of effective curriculum and instruction. Studies of organizations are providing more understanding of barriers and opportunities in stimulating and implementing innovations. Studies of schools are providing new knowledge of the impact of classroom and teaching activities. Though some of the relevant research is disciplinary, much of it is not. As we concluded in our previous report (Committee, 1985:52): "[a] thorough understanding of how children learn or fail to learn to reason will require fundamental research that involves the highest order of both disciplinary and interdisciplinary research skills."

Third, there is good reason for concern about the link between scientific research on teaching and learning and the every-day experiences of teachers and students. Research on teaching and learning is often inattentive to insights and effective practices that are well known to experienced teachers, while the practice of teaching is often inattentive to knowledge that has come from educational research. More is known about teaching and learning science and mathematics than is currently being used effectively.

Numerous terms are used to describe the various links between research and practice and among researchers from different fields and institutions, but none is fully satisfactory in the present context. Therefore, throughout this report, we use _interdisciplinary_ as a generic term to refer to all kinds of research/practice collaborations as well as the term to refer to collaboration among disciplines. Of particular interest are the following:

1. Collaboration among different specialties of a discipline or profession--for example, among cognitive, developmental, and social psychologists to understand the role of early childhood experiences in the comprehension of scientific concepts.
2. Collaboration among disciplines--for example, among chemists, educational psychologists, and cognitive scientists to structure chemical knowledge for effective instruction.
3. Collaboration among basic research, applied research, and development and application--for example, to improve the effectiveness of computer technology in the teaching of basic arithmetic operations.

4. Collaboration among practitioners, policy makers, and researchers--for example, to develop and adopt curricula and teaching materials that communicate scientific knowledge in a way that is both scientifically rigorous and educationally manageable.

THE NEED FOR COLLABORATION

The contemporary organization of science is not the result of an arbitrary division of labor; rather, it reflects the ways the structure of human understanding of knowledge has evolved through experience. Although knowledge cannot be factored into completely autonomous clusters of phenomena and variables, some things are more tightly linked than others. The disciplinary organization of research facilitates exchanges among people and ideas that have many interconnections at the expense of those that have few.

Some domains of inquiry fit less well into the disciplinary structure than others. One domain that fits badly is research on mathematics, science, and technology education. Understanding and improving education in science requires three distinct kinds of knowledge: first, the structures and processes of the subjects to be taught; second, the fundamental biological, psychological, linguistic, and sociological processes involved in learning these subjects, particularly the development of reasoning skills; and third, the contexts in which teaching and learning take place, the wide range of formal and informal instructional experiences that are, in turn, embedded in contexts of interacting social and political institutions and norms. The need for different kinds of knowledge is illustrated by the examples given in Chapter 2 of important research requiring interdisciplinary collaboration.

On the basis of the committee's earlier work, this report considers four categories of interrelated research: on mathematics and science curriculum, on teachers and teaching, on improving the settings for learning, and on change in schools. For example, research on curricula, instruction, and new learning systems includes research on the organization of knowledge and processes to be taught, on the development of reasoning skills in mathematics and science, on testing and evaluation, and on the possibilities for improvements through computer-based technologies. Much of this research requires cooperation among teachers, subject-matter specialists, educational and learning psychologists, sociologists, computer scientists, and materials developers. As another example, research on the various settings in which learning take place--the home, the classroom and school, television and other mass media, and peer groups and other informal instructors--entails collaboration between sociologists of the school and sociologists of the family, between developmental psychologists and anthropologists, between teachers and linguists, between students of organizations and developers of new information technologies.

BARRIERS TO COLLABORATION

The historical examples summarized in Chapter 3 of this report (and other examples that could be added) illustrate that it is sometimes possible to develop effective interdisciplinary efforts. A need for such work, however, does not translate reliably into a burst of productive collaboration. In large part, the problems of interdisciplinary work stem from the utility of the division of labor and the specialization in science and education. Research scientists do not wander far from their specialties precisely because society and good sense dictate that most of the time they should not do so. For the same reasons, professional educators do not wander far from their professional expertise. The difficulties of collaboration between teachers, administrators, and scientists are generated by the same attributes of organization that make them efficient in their own spheres. There are three factors that exacerbate the difficulties implicit in a specialized organization of knowledge and research: (1) problems of concern; (2) problems of organization, coordination, and communication; and (3) problems of recruitment.

Problems of Concern

Most of the major historical examples of successes in interdisciplinary collaboration resulted from an unusual level of shared concern. When there has been an overpowering sense of urgency about a problem, as in the case of some issues of national crisis (e.g., the development of the atomic bomb, the early years of the space program) or deep appeal to personal values (e.g., arms control research, research on women), it is easier to attract outstanding researchers and others to interdisciplinary collaboration and to sustain their involvement. However, there is likely to be a limit to the number of "crises" or "great opportunities" that a social system, or an individual, will accept as real at any one time.

While many people agree that the problems of mathematics, science, and technology education in contemporary America are important, they do not generate that kind of urgency or concern. Those with major concern for that education should continue to elaborate the many ways in which the problems of scientific literacy are legitimate bases for commitment, but one should not anticipate that even the most persuasive arguments will transform the problems into crisis concerns for many people.

Individual scientists may also see professional as well as personal reasons for not undertaking such work. For example, some social and behavioral scientists may hesitate to respond to a call to increase literacy in the natural sciences if success in that task is likely to lead to decreasing attention to literacy in the foundations of their own disciplines. A research physicist may have a greater stake in literacy in the physical sciences but may see her contribution to such an effort as being less significant than a publishable research result in physics. And a high school science teacher may see only modest benefit in contributing to a long-term research project when he is confronted with more pressing daily problems of teaching a class.

The fact that exceptionally effective interdisciplinary effort seems to have stemmed from exceptional conditions of shared concern is a warning not to expect miracles, but not a cause for despair. If crisis or shared values were required for all coordinated effort, there would not be much of it. Yet society routinely induces disparate individuals and groups to solve problems in a coordinated way, even without shared values or sense of crisis. The most obvious examples of such successes are found in price systems, political exchange systems, and bureaucracies. Each coordinates conflicting participants without securing agreement on values beyond a broad acceptance of the "rules of the game." They function through the design and implementation of various forms of contracts and implicit contracts, socialization into legitimate behavior through rules and roles, and the creation of coalitions.

Problems of Organization, Coordination, and Communication

The problems of organizing diversity are not fundamentally different from general problems of organization. They involve two things: a choice of the appropriate balance between gains from coordinated control of diverse activities and gains from decentralized specialization and a choice of mechanisms for achieving that balance efficiently. In general, although efficient mechanisms minimize the costs, there is always a trade-off between investing effort in coordinating activities and investing effort in improving specialized diversity. When activities are heavily interdependent, coordination seems particularly appropriate; when they are not, decentralized specialization seems better.

It is easier to describe the trade-offs involved in organizing diversity than to find the appropriate balance. Many proposed interdisciplinary projects face skepticism and resistance from researchers in particular disciplines. Part of this response is undoubtedly due to the fact that the benefits from such research are likely to be less salient to them than to outsiders, but it is also attributable to a greater awareness of the difficulties. An interdisciplinary project that requires extensive cross-fertilization of ideas at the level of the individual research worker incurs heavy costs of organization, communication, and coordination. Indeed, persons within individual disciplines often see the difficulties of fitting different perspectives together and recognize the cost of coordination and communication more clearly than do those outside the individual disciplines, who may see the need for cross-disciplinary, multispecialty, multiperspective projects, but tend to underestimate the organizational costs of doing them. Since such people are more likely to be found in managerial positions and in funding agencies, there is a persistent tendency for the organizational costs (both in money and in time) to be underfunded.

Problems of Recruitment

Finding ways to stimulate interdisciplinary activity may not be easy, but it is easier than ensuring that the people recruited for those activities are talented enough to meet the challenge of the research. For some of the people most needed, participation in interdisciplinary projects is arguably both less socially efficient and less personally attractive than work in more specialized activities. Talented scientists with an absolute advantage over others for a particular project often have a comparative advantage in their disciplinary work as well. And interdisciplinary research may not be attractive to them, particularly in the early stages of their careers, because of the incentive structure of scientific careers and the role definitions of disciplinary scientists. The rewards of a scientific career lie mainly within a discipline; recognition by one's peers is essential and comes primarily for disciplinary excellence. Similarly, an experienced and talented lawyer, physician, teacher, or administrator is unlikely to find multiperspective activities either as consistent with role definitions or as rewarding as staying within relatively circumscribed professional activities and groups. This situation argues the need to create incentives for interdisciplinary research that counterbalance the existing adverse reward system.

Aside from rewards, serious interdisciplinary work tends to be painful. Interdisciplinary collaboration involves situations in which roles, reputations, and paradigms have to be renegotiated or redefined. The process is likely to make participants uncomfortable, particularly if they are relatively successful in a discipline or specialty. The excitement of uncertainty is a classical basis for the excitement of science, but the uncertainties that attract research scientists are characteristically within sharply defined constraints of established paradigms. Economists think like economists; chemists think like chemists. Research within a single paradigm is more easily designed, executed, interpreted, and communicated than is research that involves more than one. Yet the intellectual challenges inherent in many of the problems that require the expertise of more than one specialty have attracted some of the finest scientific minds to interdisciplinary research, leading to the creation of whole new fields, such as astrophysics, molecular biology, and cognitive science. However, it takes established scientists, with tenure and solid self-esteem, to take up the challenge. This implies that interdisciplinary research requires the leadership of senior scientists and cannot ordinarily succeed by attracting just junior researchers, however talented. At the same time, even the best disciplinary scientists will, on average, be less competent at interdisciplinary work than they are in their disciplines. Though they may be more competent than most others at interdisciplinary work, they will have to learn about somewhat unfamiliar problems, people, language, standards, and techniques. Unless it is possible simply to import a particular paradigm into a new field, interdisciplinary efforts are relatively difficult in execution as well as relatively uncertain in outcome.

These problems are particularly notable when, as is often true in education, the impetus for interdisciplinary collaboration comes from outside the field. There are two difficulties with imposing an interdisciplinary focus from a funding agency or manager. The first is the obvious one that the best researchers prefer to work on problems of their own choosing and are in short enough supply to be able to do so. The second is that outsiders often lack clarity about the task, which, when added to the other confusions of interdisciplinary work, gives such work low prospect of success.

Yet there are occasions when interdisciplinary work is not only appropriate but also appealing: when the normal research activities of a disciplinary scientist lead to important questions unanswerable within that discipline; when a teacher sees a need for greater comprehension of some specific feature of the learning process; or when a policy analyst wants advice on a well-defined problem of learning technology. In such cases each is recruited relatively easily into an interdisciplinary project.

OVERCOMING THE BARRIERS TO COLLABORATION

The committee believes that a coherent attack on the problem of encouraging good interdisciplinary collaboration is possible. The first requirement is to have talented people within each relevant specialty help define the interdisciplinary problems to be worked on. The second requirement is to recognize that the primary barrier to such collaboration is the fundamental efficiency of the division of labor and specialization: since specialization serves so well most of the time, it is difficult to organize along different lines when the traditional division of labor serves poorly. Such a recognition implies that the fundamental strategy for encouraging relevant interdisciplinary collaboration involves working within and around the disciplinary and professional structures rather than attempting a basic reconstruction of the organization of science and education.

First, staying power is needed to make a real difference in science, mathematics, and technology education. Therefore, any agency sponsoring research and development in this area needs to institute a systematic procedure for establishing program goals, tracking program effects in relation to goals over time, and making adjustments to improve program effectiveness. Our additional suggestions cover each of the three problems identified above.

Ameliorating the Problems of Concern

We believe there are three different ways by which the problems of inadequate concern can be confronted: creating a general sense of crisis; identifying a subgroup of relevant people who, for particularistic reasons, are more concerned than the average scientist; and substituting other mechanisms for the motivational cohesion produced through shared concern. Specifically, a systematic program might be created, directed toward the scientific community, explaining the magnitude of the problems within mathematics, science, and technology education and indicating the importance of interdisciplinary collaborative efforts to confront those problems. Such a program might address the scientific community in general or identify subgroups of scientists and others with particular concerns about education. Also, more careful consideration needs to be given to the various aspects of problems requiring interdisciplinary work in order to minimize the costs of collaboration and communication. For example, an agency could ask a small interdisciplinary team to identify components of direct relevance to a given interdisciplinary problem but that can be addressed within the boundaries of one discipline or specialty before being coordinated with other pieces of the work.

Ameliorating the Problems of Organization, Communication, and Coordination

We believe that the problems of organization, communication, and coordination reflect primarily a tendency to underestimate the costs of interdisciplinary collaboration, particularly as the number of perspectives involved increases. We suggest a more careful consideration by funding agencies of the relation between the marginal cost of adding additional perspectives to a project and the marginal return. The tendency to think if it is good to add one additional perspective it must be better to add four needs to be tempered by a recognition that the costs of organization, communication, and coordination roughly double with each new specialty. Successful collaboration typically involves a relatively small number of perspectives. Also, sponsoring agencies need to make a special effort to provide adequate funding for the extra costs of interdisciplinary projects and commit themselves to program and resource stability. Tempting as it is to reorganize programs as educational priorities replace each other, successful interdisciplinary collaboration takes time to build. One way of providing time and adequate funding is to estabish research or demonstration centers in which experts from various specialties work together on joint projects; however, the design and management of such centers must be carefully thought through in light of experience with such centers in education and in other fields.

A possible programmatic initiative might be for the National Science Foundation again to provide funding explicitly for interdisciplinary research, as in the joint National Institute on Education/National Science Foundation program of 1981-1982. Other possibilities include a special program to fund the interaction of researchers with common interests and complementary training, including support for sabbaticals or lengthy visits to encourage collaborative projects. With more ambition, one might consider developing an entity like the Center for Advanced Study in the Behavioral Sciences at which scholars with differing backgrounds can work together on common education problems. These and other program alternatives are discussed in Chapter 4.

Ameliorating the Problems of Recruitment

We believe it is relatively easy to stimulate interdisciplinary work, but it is hard to ensure that the individuals led to engage in that work will be of a quality commensurate with the difficulty of an interdisciplinary task. The primary mechanisms for recruiting talented people are the selection of challenging problems and the provision of attractive incentives for interdisciplinary collaboration. In order to be effective in attracting the desired participation, such incentives must be tailored to a well-defined interdisciplinary task that is recognized as critical to solving problems having a high priority for outstanding individuals within a specialty.

The Foundation should consider a program of grants that first identifies individuals whose contribution to improving mathematics, science, and technology education would be particularly critical and then asks them to identify an interdisciplinary effort that (a) is socially important, (b) would have a high prospect of success, and (c) would secure their attention because of its intellectual challenge and scientific excitement. An alternative is the identification, through special conferences or advisory groups, of interdisciplinary problems that have strong linkages, either through theory or application, to existing discipline-based research, so that researchers could perceive opportunities for contributing to education without necessarily changing their field. A third possibility is a program of grants and fellowships that will encourage able young scientists and educators to acquire the tools of another specialty and enable established professionals to provide leadership for interdisciplinary research. Chapter 4 provides further suggestions on pertinent program alternatives.

2
Research Needs in Science and Mathematics Education

Improving the quality of teaching and learning in mathematics, science, and technology is a problem with many dimensions. In the last 20 years progress has been made in developing a basis for better education in science, mathematics, and technology. Experimentation with curriculum content and instructional strategies has yielded valuable insights. Cognitive studies are providing more understanding of the nature of learning and effective instruction. Organizational studies have identified barriers and opportunities in implementing change in schools. Advances in the basic disciplines of the sciences and mathematics and in information engineering provide new resources for curriculum and instruction.

In this chapter the needs of mathematics and science education are considered, together with a set of research goals to meet those needs. The discussion is organized around four areas: the mathematics and science curriculum, the knowledge and skills of teachers, settings for learning, and change in schools. Though some of the research goals pertinent to these areas are well served through work within specific disciplines, others require collaboration among several disciplines and between research and practice. Examples of needed interdisciplinary research are outlined, drawn in part from the committee's preceding report (Committee, 1985), to illustrate their potential contribution to progress in science and mathematics education.

THE MATHEMATICS AND SCIENCE CURRICULUM

Current curricula and instructional practices have evolved through a slow process of accretion of goals, educational experience, institutional mechanisms, and organizational behaviors. For example, biology as a 10th-grade course was institutionalized in the 1920s (Moyer and Mayer, 1985). Schools consider changing long-established practices only if alternatives can be demonstrated to be superior. Patience and persistence is needed for the development of such alternatives, for demonstrating their effectiveness through exemplary programs in a variety of school settings, and for the process of adoption and adaptation that enables their installation in enough appropriate sites to make a difference in education.

The committee identified three curriculum-related areas that are likely to profit from interdisciplinary research and development: (1) improving the teaching of reasoning and understanding and the context of instruction; (2) introducing new content into science and mathematics curricula; and (3) developing linkages between curriculum and testing.

Improving Instruction

Teaching Reasoning and Understanding

A critical problem with the mathematics curriculum in grades K-12 and the science curriculum in grades 7-12 is too much emphasis on facts and too little emphasis on basic concepts and methods of mathematical and scientific reasoning. As for the science curriculum in elementary school, it hardly exists, and where it does, it is more often a reading program about science or an eclectic selection of "science projects" rather than an organized science program.

The problem of too much rote learning and too little teaching for understanding also exists at the level of introductory college courses (Arons, 1981, 1983)--the only science courses most teachers take to prepare for teaching. And teachers teach as they are taught. They also use the textbook as their central instructional tool (Stake and Easley, 1978). Analysis of current science textbooks has documented that the learning of special or technical vocabulary, i.e., rote memorization, is a central feature of these texts (Yager, 1983). It should not be surprising that recent studies on the overall outcomes of schooling show gains in elementary knowledge and skills by younger students--the "basics" the schools have been stressing--but that higher-level processes are being acquired less well (Champagne and Klopfer, 1977; National Assessment of Educational Progress, 1983a). Not only do schools emphasize the learning of facts, but the current methods of presenting science and mathematics appear to alienate female children and minority children of both sexes, who often decide in elementary school and again at the junior high level that these subjects are not for them.

Although research to date has not fully explained how young children develop scientific reasoning and conceptual knowledge, powerful levers are available for the improvement of curriculum and instruction. One is the advance of cognitive and instructional sciences, areas that were just emerging 25 years ago. The knowledge base they have created permits the development of instructional materials and systems that can facilitate the learning of concepts and skills now largely absent in mathematics and science education. Also, current technological developments are stimulating application of new understandings about cognitive learning to mathematics and science: see, for example, the discussion in the committee's previous report of the work by Larkin and Reif (1976); Anderson (1981); Riley et al. (1983); Schoenfeld (1979); Champagne et al. (1980); Clement (1982); and McCloskey (1983). Such research has produced better understanding of the components that make good instruction effective, which include: (a) models of correct performance (e.g., of physics or mathematics problem-solving), (b) models of uninstructed performance (e.g., "preconceptions" of scientific phenomena that interact with theories being taught), and (c) models of effective instruction (e.g., principles of design for effective instruction).

It appears that problem-solving, comprehension, and effective reasoning are based on subject-specific knowledge. Therefore, it seems best to teach reasoning skills in the context of specific subjects that students are learning. This finding implies that research on reasoning needs to involve experts in a particular discipline as well as cognitive scientists and experienced teachers. As an example, sustained collaborative work involving physicists and cognitive scientists has produced an effective means of teaching beginning students the difficult problem-solving techniques required for exploiting Newton's laws (Reif and Heller, 1982).

In summary, to solve the problem of presenting scientific and mathematics subject matter in ways that enhance understanding and knowledge about natural phenomena and build competence in quantitative thinking requires the involvement of cognitive scientists, scholars in the scientific and mathematical disciplines, teachers, designers and developers, and computer experts.

The Context of Instruction

Advanced scholarship in a subject is based on theories and concepts that make a domain accessible to subject-matter experts. However, a theory for the expert may not be good as a pedagogical theory for the novice. Recent work in cognitive psychology has described how acquired knowledge is organized and represented and how cognitive models can facilitate reasoning and thinking as students use and test these models to solve problems and revise what they already know (Estes et al., 1982; Rumelhart and Norman, 1981; Resnick, 1987), but such research has had little influence on the rigidly hierarchical conception of science and mathematics that undergirds most classroom instruction. However, effective teachers use their experience on how students learn to shape the subject matter they present (Brophy and Evertson, 1976; Collins and Stevens, 1982). This craft knowledge provides an important source for developing instructional theory for teaching science and mathematics to students at different levels of competence and education.

Another source of knowledge is research on how young children learn (Istomina, 1975; Donaldson, 1978; DeLoache and Brown, 1979; Carey, 1985). This research suggests that a fundamental way of changing how much time a child takes for a particular task is to change the context of the task by embedding it in some larger activity involving familiar situations. Knowledge is lacking on how the insights gained from the work with young children can be applied at higher levels of the curriculum in the areas of science, mathematics, and technology. However, there is evidence that science curricula combining activity-based instruction with appropriate text materials are more effective than traditional curricula in teaching higher-order skills (Shymansky et al., 1983; Holdzkom and Lutz, 1984).

Because of the great importance of curricular orientation and context to the learning of mathematics, science, and technology, the committee urges special emphasis on this research area. Priorities include research on how important tasks can be embedded in contexts that reduce time needed for learning; under what circumstances and in what ways hands-on experience and laboratory experiments as well as models based on systematic laws can be used to enhance learning; and what makes theory-oriented instruction work. The kinds of collaboration needed to carry out this sort of work, since it is more applied, are even broader than those required for developing a better understanding of reasoning processes and will require--in addition to subject matter experts, cognitive scientists, computer experts, and experienced teachers--the involvement of sociologists, psychologists, and anthropologists.

Integrating New Content Areas

Educating for Scientific Literacy

The goal of elementary science education should be to prepare children to understand science and mathematics, to teach them a few representative concepts, to acquaint them with abstraction, and to introduce them to scientific reasoning and the nature of scientific evidence. The temptation to include "the most important basic concepts" in each scientific discipline probably needs to be resisted, because the list will soon be very long. In the committee's view, it is more important for students to learn a few concepts well, with sufficient understanding to teach the concept to another person, than to have superficial exposure to many concepts. True understanding will make it much easier for students to master additional concepts later and will make science enjoyable rather than intimidating.

The secondary school curriculum needs to address the goal of improving scientific literacy for all students (National Science Foundation, 1983). School leavers, no matter when they stop their education, need to find employment in a labor market increasingly driven by technological innovation. For everyone, an understanding of the scientific method, of the ways in which inferences are drawn from evidence, of the nature of controlled experiments and scientific proof will be essential for making individual and public choices in coming decades.

A general conceptual understanding will be more useful than a small amount of specific, technical knowledge that soon will be out of date. People will also need a continuing capability for learning and comprehension of science and mathematics throughout life. Consequently, curriculum and instructional alternatives must be concerned with methods of learning that prepare people to take advantage of the life-long availability of information technology.

Curricula depend upon and are built around educational materials. Textbooks are a central factor in determining what is learned on what time schedule (Stake and Easley, 1978). The content of textbooks is influenced by their authors' sense of appropriate learning goals, the publishers' perception of the demands of the education market, and the priorities and procedures for textbook approval and selection of states and local school districts. Neither scientists from the disciplines taught in school nor cognitive scientists have been much involved in the process in recent years. In contrast, the attempts to reform mathematics and science curricula in the late 1950s and 1960s (see Chapter 3) did involve scientists and mathematicians, and much attention was paid to the balance between emphasis on facts and emphasis on concepts and learning how to learn. Though the then new curricula often were difficult for students and mismatched to teachers' competencies, particularly in the elementary grades, they led to some improvement in the learning of inferential and critical thinking skills (Shymansky et al., 1983). However, those curricula have been replaced by more traditional materials, and the effects have not been maintained.

The other component of teaching science, hands-on experience in elementary school and laboratory experiments in the upper grades, is in danger of disappearing from many schools. At the same time, the potential of computers to strengthen science and mathematics education remains largely untapped. The educational computer software that is commercially available shows little of the creativity of pilot programs developed by scientists working with cognitive researchers.

A concerted interdisciplinary research effort is needed to improve the science and mathematics curricula and their use. First, scientists and learning specialists must agree on the appropriate content for development of higher-order skills. Second, new subject-matter content within various fields and at various grade levels must be explored as potentially more appropriate than traditional topics. As a specific instance, systematic attention must be given to changes in the knowledge structures and the processes of the sciences and mathematics as a result of readily available computation and the implications of these changes for the school curriculum. Just as the advent of calculators made traditional drill in using logarithm tables superfluous, the advent of more powerful computers has implications for all the science and mathematics courses taught in school. Third, the substantive content in current textbooks and software must be reformulated to support the learning of reasoning, thinking, and problem-solving skills as well as lower-order recall and memorization tasks. And fourth, curriculum design must take into account the role of hands-on experience and the laboratory in the learning of science. Each of these efforts involves the cooperation of several disciplines and specialties.

Technology Education

In addition to these research issues on curriculum content for science and mathematics, there are specific questions surrounding two aspects of technology education: the subject matter appropriate to understanding technological systems and the teaching of computer science. Unlike the more traditional domains of science and mathematics, technology and computer science do not have well-established curricula. With respect to understanding technological systems (as contrasted to the basic science that gives rise to them), the traditional school curriculum is essentially a blank.

With respect to computer science, many schools are now introducing "computer literacy" courses. Some districts are even requiring such a course for high school graduation. Often, such courses focus on teaching programming in a particular computer language. In other instances, computer literacy courses deal with the capabilities and functioning of computers, either with or without hands-on experience, and may include topics on the effects of computers on the workplace and society. Knowledge is lacking about the age and grade levels at which computers and programming should be introduced and about the effects of alternative curricula in computer literacy.

Interdisciplinary research is needed to provide characterizations of the cognitive skills and knowledge needed for understanding of and successful performance in technological systems and to develop usable school curricula in this area and in computer literacy.

Vocational Education

A special case in the school curriculum that involves both scientific literacy and technology education is the relationship of vocational instruction to the conventional mathematics and science experience in elementary and secondary schools. As work in industry entailing computers and robots becomes extensive, the boundaries between vocational and academic learning will become ever more blurred. Employers are increasingly concerned with instruction in technical matters that involves some combination of apprenticeship, vocational training, and precollege academic learning. One of the unresolved questions is how and where these learning activities should be provided--in schools, in industry, or some combination of industry and schools. For example, in a 1984 survey the Industrial Research Institute identified some 161 cooperative ventures betweem its member industrial research laboratories and high schools and colleges that emphasize mathematics, science, and technology training in practical settings. As of 1983, nearly 2 out of 3 of the nation's major companies were involved in cooperative programs or provided internships for students from local schools (Lund and McGuire, 1984). Interdisciplinary research projects could utilize the existing collaborative education and training ventures to assess their potential for instruction in science and mathematics and in various vocations.

Curriculum and Testing

Most present classroom methods of testing what students know emphasize the recall of facts--as does most teaching. If tests are not to trivialize instruction even further, new approaches to assessing student achievement must be developed that aim at conceptual understanding, the ability to reason and think with scientific or mathematical subject matter, and competence in the key processes that characterize science or mathematics (Frederiksen, 1984; Romberg, 1986).

Work on two different kinds of tests is needed. Assessments of student achievement that reflect the expectations of the life-long social and economic roles of an individual need to be developed. And more limited tests that bear on the curriculum of a particular grade or course need improvement. States or school districts should be assisted in developing tests that measure student reasoning and problem-solving skills. If more adequate tests were available, school district evaluations and certifications could be tied to overall test scores as well as to patterns of variance in achievement across social class, race, language, gender, and economic characteristics of pupils. Thus, test outcomes would be directly related to what a school is expected to achieve, and test results would have meaningful impact on the schools.

There is a new and promising line of research that links traditional psychometrics to the growing understanding of reasoning skills (Hunt et al., 1973; Glaser, 1981; Sternberg, 1977, 1984). Cheap, powerful computers provide possibilities for more effective interactive testing--making tests more accurate and less time-consuming for students as well as less labor-intensive for those administering them (Weiss, 1983)--but further research is required to explore those possibilities.

Tests play a role in the learning process itself. They tell students what in the curriculum is important and shape the teaching and learning process (Frederiksen, 1984; Romberg, 1986). If, for example, testing is confined to recalling facts, students will concentrate on memorizing those facts, ignoring the more sophisticated levels of understanding and reasoning to which teachers and text materials may be rendering lip service. Teachers and school administrators also use tests as a guide to curriculum emphasis, especially when student performance on given tests is used as a measure of teacher and school performance.

Research needs in testing include the development of practical tests that reliably assess reasoning ability, possibly using interactive testing made possible by microcomputers; improving the testing of mathematics and science achievement to reflect important instructional goals and objectives; and techniques for educating teachers to become better writers of test questions, particularly of questions that test for higher-order intellectual skills and levels of learning. Cognitive scientists, psychologists, mathematicians, physicists, chemists, and biologists must all be involved in such efforts.

THE KNOWLEDGE AND SKILLS OF TEACHERS

Teachers must understand the material they are presenting in order to teach it effectively. The natural curiosity of children leads them to ask basic questions. This tendency will be encouraged by teachers who understand basic concepts themselves and who can use this understanding to lead students to a comprehension of fundamental ideas of physics, chemistry, biology, and mathematics. Subject-matter understanding is essential because it allows a teacher to use whatever examples are at hand to show students how evidence is used to build knowledge. Furthermore, a teacher must understand the nature of scientific reasoning and know the difference between evidence and inference. Teachers must also understand how students acquire knowledge and understanding in science and mathematics. New curricula and teaching materials will be useless without teacher understanding.

The committee has identified three areas that would benefit greatly by interdisciplinary research on science and mathematics teaching: (1) the content of teacher education; (2) elementary teachers' knowledge and understanding; and (3) assessment of initiatives related to the teaching profession.

Content of Teacher Education

Subject-matter courses taken by prospective teachers --usually the standard courses offered by science departments--often cover too much content at too rapid a pace and seldom pay explicit heed to developing reasoning capacities (Arons, 1983). Hence, prospective and practicing teachers often lack a genuine understanding of concepts and lines of reasoning that characterize the subject(s) they are teaching and, having missed effective training themselves, are unable to cultivate and enhance the basic reasoning capacity of their students. Thus, additional teacher understanding of science cannot be achieved simply by sending teachers back to the universities to take a few more science courses. Moreover, methods courses in education are not very helpful in elucidating how students learn specific subject matter, because these courses do not often include recent advances in the cognitive sciences. Thus, courses in the universities, whether located in schools of education or in the disciplinary departments, are inadequate to train teachers in science and mathematics education.

Teacher competence involves adequate cognitive mastery of the subject matter to be taught and, in the case of science, proficiency in handling experimental materials that can lead students to form new concepts from observation and evidence. Even the best curricula will be ineffective unless teachers are trained to deal with various modes of abstract reasoning, for example: the logic of arithmetic involved in ratios and division, the logic of control of variables, dealing with propositional statements, recognizing gaps in available information, making inferences and predictions from mental models, doing hypothetico-deductive reasoning, and the like (Arons, 1981). In fact, the processes and problems involved in educating teachers to acquire these capacities are not very different from those involved for younger learners.

New undergraduate and in-service courses that emphasize conceptual learning and comprehension in science and mathematics need to be designed. What is needed is not only new course development, but also new educational research oriented toward specific subject matter. Cognitive scientists and subject-matter scientists must collaborate in studying how scientific knowledge is acquired by older students, i.e., prospective or practicing teachers. Communication between these groups for the purpose of teacher education has been minimal up until now, but it must be increased. And both sides will have to master knowledge of the other discipline if they are to collaborate fruitfully in research on scientific learning and in developing improved courses useful for teacher education.

Elementary Teachers' Knowledge and Understanding

Conventional views of public education presume that the teachers of elementary school science and mathematics understand the subjects sufficiently well to transfer comprehension to the great diversity of students they face in the classroom. Evidence from teacher examinations (Vobejda, 1985), and research on teacher performance and student achievement (Schalock, 1979; Fisher et al., 1980; Leinhardt and Greeno, 1984; Lampert, 1986) does not bear out this presumption. Assessments of teacher performance should take into account teachers' perceptions of how and what students are learning and teachers' ability to recognize the failure to learn. Thus, teacher education would concentrate on the relatively new area of teachers' interpretation of students' thought processes and ability to use new skills rather than traditional estimates of factual knowledge. To develop such education, further investigations by subject-matter experts in mathematics and science and behavioral and cognitive scientists are needed on whether and how teachers effect student learning.

One approach to improving mathematics and science learning in elementary school in the use of specialist teachers. Specialized teaching, starting in grades 4 or 5, characterizes the education systems of many other industrialized nations, particularly those in which students outperform U.S. students. A few such specialist teachers work in selected school districts in several states, but at present the practice is uncommon in U.S. elementary schools. If the use of specialist teachers were to spread in grades 4-6, what training would be appropriate for them? How could school systems use specialist teachers without the investment of additional resources that may not be available? What should be the role of the specialist teacher: student contact? working with regular grade teachers? both? Cooperative efforts involving several specialties from the natural and social sciences as well as experienced teachers and administrators are needed to develop better approaches to the education of those who teach mathematics and science in the elementary grades, whether they are specialist or regular teachers.

Initiatives to Improve the Teaching Profession

Many of the current initiatives for improving education are aimed at making teaching a more rigorous profession. Thus, 32 states have changed teacher certification requirements, 28 states have changed teacher education curricula, and 20 states have raised entrance requirements for teacher education programs (Goertz et al., 1984). Other policies that have been proposed are to require liberal arts majors for all teachers and a 5-year rather than 4-year degree program (Scannel and Guenther,

1981; Boyer, 1983; National Commission for Excellence in Teacher Education, 1984; Holmes Group, 1986; Carnegie Forum on Education and the Economy, 1986), and to ensure teacher competence through a nationally recognized licensing examination (Shanker, 1985). Still other proposals are intended to make precollege education a more attractive profession in order to encourage entry into teaching of individuals of high ability and keep competent teachers and administrators from leaving the schools. These proposals include salary increases and structural changes in compensation for teachers and the creation of more conducive working conditions in schools.

Few of the policy changes that have been implemented are based on research evidence about the decisions of individuals to enter teaching (Murnane, 1985) or the acquisition of knowledge and skills deemed necessary for science and mathematics teaching. Some of the new policies may prove effective; others may have some undesirable consequences. For example, Summers and Wolfe (1977) found a statistically significant negative correlation between teachers' scores on the National Teachers Exam and their students' test score gains. Possibly more critical than initial certification--the object of many of the policy changes--is recertification, since specific college learning, even if pertinent to teaching, fades unless used and renewed. A 3-year cycle of evaluation for recertification might be considered, during which teachers would be asked to produce their own evidence on their competence.

The current experimentation with incentives, teacher education programs, and credentialing sharpens the need to understand better (a) who gets access to various teacher preparation programs, (b) the content of these programs, (c) the regulation of access to teaching positions, and (d) the maintenance of teacher competence. These factors are poorly understood even for the current pool of teachers. Gaining a better understanding will require cooperative work by economists, sociologists, subject-matter specialists, teacher educators, and educational administrators.

SETTINGS FOR LEARNING

What factors influence students' willingness or interest in learning science and mathematics? To what extent do experiences in the elementary grades influence choice of courses at the secondary level and later careers? Research suggests that the school environment, family, and community all influence students' attitudes and confidence in their own abilities to comprehend science and mathematics.

Three areas in this domain appear particularly in need of interdisciplinary research: (1) assessing the effects of school and classroom settings; (2) understanding parental effects on student learning; and (3) examining educational models that cross institutional boundaries.

School and Classroom Settings

Schools should be responsible for motivating students. The success of some schools in improving the performance or commitment of students should be studied to learn how schools can persuade students that scientific literacy, like learning to read, is expected of all. Research points to a number of questions that need to be addressed (see reviews by Chipman and Thomas, 1984; Chipman et al., 1985; Eccles-Parsons et al., 1983; American Association for the Advancement of Science, 1984). How does the school environment influence the perception that science and mathematics are difficult? Are teacher expectations and attitudes or institutional expectations influential? Do the different reactions of different cultural and gender groups to science and mathematics result at least in part from the attitudes of teachers and school administrators toward them? How should schools and classrooms be organized for effective learning of mathematics and science?

Schools organize classrooms in various ways (Bidwell and Kasarda, 1975). Group placement based on ability is common to reduce heterogeneity and match instruction to the students' skills. Such placement has been shown to be stable over time--once in the low group, it is hard to get out--and to have differential impact on high- and low-group students. Studies consistently and robustly document that ability grouping has detrimental effects within classrooms on average and low-ability groups (Persell, 1977; Good and Marshall, 1984). Inappropriate grouping may amplify relatively minor differences at the beginning of 1st grade into major differences in later grades; it certainly affects students' perceptions about their ability to do mathematics and science (Hallinan and Sorensen, 1984).

Successful methods of classroom instruction frequently involve breaking classes into smaller activity groups that combine theoretical understanding with hands-on familiarity. Unfortunately, these conditions have only been maintained in specialized programs (Goodlad, 1984; Hawkins and Sheingold, 1983; Moll and Diaz, 1982; Peterson et al., 1984). Even programs with demonstrated success, like the activity-based elementary school science curricula of the 1960s, currently languish and are used only when individual teachers make heroic efforts or an especially well-educated parent group creates a demand. Therefore, research is needed on how to make student activity groups successful, especially in multi-ethnic classrooms, over a range of mathematics and science tasks. In particular, the combined effects of curriculum, school organization, teacher training, and small-group dynamics--especially the question of group heterogeneity--need to be better understood. That kind of research requires not only subject-matter experts and cognitive scientists, but also sociologists, anthropologists, and social psychologists who have studied the environments of classrooms and whole schools.

Another important area of research concerns the relation between time used for instruction and student learning. A recent study by Stevenson et al. (1986) showed that the mathematics achievement of American children compared with the achievement of Japanese and Chinese children consistently declined from 1st through 5th grades, and that differences in the amount of instructional time and direct instruction by the teacher appear to be important factors. In the 5th grade, American children spend 64.5 percent of their classroom time involved in academic activities; Chinese children spend 91.5 percent and Japanese children spend 87.4 percent. American teachers spent proportionally less time during the school day on the subject matter (21 percent) than did the Chinese teachers (58 percent) or the Japanese teachers (33 percent). The Chinese and Japanese children also spent a considerably larger portion of the school day on mathematics than did the American children, who averaged less than 20 percent of the school day on mathematics.

School organizational factors that affect teachers' use of time, such as staff support and professional autonomy, and factors that increase or decrease teacher incentives and motivation to improve their teaching must be better understood before interventions to increase teacher effort can be designed.

Parental Effects on Student Learning

The values, attitudes, and beliefs of American parents are important elements in how much and how well American children learn. Parental attitudes appear to make a difference for both minority and other students and for males and females (Gemill et al., 1982). A review of research on gender and mathematics (Fox, 1977) shows that support and encouragement from parents is crucial to participation in mathematics, but that parents give less encouragement to their daughters than to their sons. A survey on science done in conjunction with the National Assessment of Educational Progress (NAEP) (Hueftle et al., 1983) found that American female students were less likely to participate in science-related activities at home than were males. Females watched fewer science programs on television, read fewer books on science, and were less likely to work on science projects or hobbies. Several analyses suggest that the presence of educational resources in the home facilitates learning (e.g., Walberg et al., 1981; Rakow, 1984), but resources matter only if they are used.

Research on student learning in different countries provides insight into the importance of parental influences. American elementary students spend far less time on homework than Japanese and Chinese students (Stevenson et al., 1986; Fetters et al., 1983; Walberg et al., n. d.). For example, in the 5th grade, American mothers estimated that their children spent 46 minutes a day on homework; for the Chinese, the estimate was 114 minutes and for the Japanese, 57 minutes. At the same time, however, 69 percent of American mothers believed the small amount of homework of their children was "just right," and the Chinese and Japanese mothers were not dissatisfied with larger amounts of homework assigned to their children (Stevenson et al., 1986). Troost (1985) also found that Japanese parents have a high participation rate in schools and that parents and schools are consistent in placing high demands on students. American students receive less assistance from parents than students in China and Japan; a lower percentage have desks in the home, and fewer receive mathematics or science workbooks from parents (Stevenson et al., 1986).

Mothers in different countries have different perceptions about the factors important in student achievement: Japanese mothers assigned the highest ranking to the child's effort; American mothers gave the highest ranking to ability. The critical role of effort in achieving success, as perceived in Japan, no doubt contributes to the development of after-school schools (juku) and greater time spent by Japanese parents discussing school work with their children (Fetters et al., 1983; Stevenson et al., 1986).

Research on the home in relationship to mathematics, science, and technology education has provided some important insights, but it is limited in several respects. Variables selected for analysis and the measures of these variables vary considerably among research studies, and many fail to look simultaneously at both home and non-home influences. Also, most of the studies relating parental and home influence to achievement use tests of basic skills; possibly, the result would be different if tests of reasoning were used instead. Moreover, the studies seldom examine how effects of home and parents differ for various groups of students. Cooperative efforts will be needed among researchers who have been working from the perspectives of their own specialities. A theoretical framework must be constructed that relates critical variables pertaining to parental and home influence to different types of learning outcomes specifically in science and mathematics; effects for different segments of the student population need to be disaggregated by age, ability, ethnic group, and type of school district; and studies should distinguish factors associated with the home from those in the wider community (e.g., influences of peers, neighborhoods, mass media) but examine their interactions and joint effects on the learning of mathematics and science.

Educational Models That Cross Institutional Boundaries

Research reviewed in the paper on contextual factors in education prepared for the committee (Cole and Griffin, 1987) makes it clear that coordinated attention should be given to educational activities that cross the boundaries between school and out-of-school learning. For example, after-school learning activities could effectively increase active learning time for mathematics and science, using such settings as community centers, churches, libraries, and school facilities themselves. A variety of prototypes that suggest the range of possible activities and institutional arrangements already exists (Moll and Diaz, 1982; Woodson, 1982). What does not exist and needs interdisciplinary research to develop is an overall understanding of the potential and limitations of different configurations and sponsorships for such activities. Joint school-community programs and school-museum programs (Fantini and Sinclair, 1985) also hold promise for mathematics and science education.

The American Association for the Advancement of Science (1984) summarized a large number of exemplary educational programs serving women and minorities. The report includes much informal knowledge based on practical experience with educational programs that are successful with these populations. Many of the programs exhibit a key structural property--they create a system of education that is integrated both vertically (from early education through later years) and horizontally (they coordinate and draw support from a range of departments, institutions, and bureaucracies). For example, the Community Educational Resource and Research Center of the University of California, San Diego, brings adults, college students, and high school students into a single activity setting after school, creating vertical integration. Horizontal integration is achieved by involving multiple parties: university, school system, community.

The problem with such boundary-crossing systems, even when they are demonstrated successes, is that they are difficult to fit into existing bureaucratic arrangements. As the AAAS report notes, demonstrations of success based upon short-term funding of experiments does not ensure continuation by the sponsoring institutions. Innovative educational successes have had long-term failure built into them (American Association for the Advancement of Science, 1984; Stage et al., 1985). This history suggests a need for analysis on how to create mixed institutional systems for mathematics and science education that can be sustained in the face of existing bureaucratic and social structures.

CHANGE IN SCHOOLS

Although structural and professional aspects of schools appear to work against significant educational change, some schools achieve sizable and lasting improvements in science and mathematics teaching. What are the structural features of those schools that encourage educational reform? How did the desired improvements take place?

General research on change in organizations suggests that both the mix of organizations and the character of individual organizations change over time, but that those changes are not ordinarily attributable to the fore-sighted intention of organizational leaders (March and Simon, 1958; Cyert and March, 1963; Cohen and March, 1974). Rather, they reflect birth and growth of different organizational forms (Greiner, 1972; Kimberly and Miles, 1980), incremental trial-by-trial learning from experience (Herriott et al., 1985), and diffusion of ideas (Rogers, 1962). Education organizations, for example, respond to the pressures exerted by interest groups and emerging societal issues rather than in accord with plans and initiatives of governing boards or administrators (Dreeben, 1976; March, 1981; Cusick, 1983).

Research is needed to pinpoint those aspects of schools or school systems that work for or against educational reform. As noted, few elementary schools retained the hands-on science experiences recommended in the curriculum reforms of the 1960s. Was this important and valuable facet of science teaching dropped because of funding problems, space limitations, class size, teacher attitudes, or administrative attitudes? What is happening to laboratory instruction in high school science courses? Why? Why are computers being so little used in effective and imaginative ways for science and mathematics teaching?

Models for Change in Schools

To foster development of capabilities for change, NSF should consider supporting the design and pilot implementation of modified kinds of schooling to serve as interpretive models for effective education. These models should be designed and implemented in existing school districts in order to demonstrate what kind of capability is needed and how it can be created. In addition, basic research is needed to identify major organizational and social factors affecting change within educational institutions. A research program should examine factors affecting the generation of new alternatives for mathematics, science, and technology instruction and learning; the dissemination of information about such alternatives and experience with them; incentives within educational systems for considering and adopting new alternatives; and capabilities for implementing effective new alternatives. To avoid the presumption that change is always good, a research program should also consider both the conditions under which educational institutions fail to adopt effective new programs or methods and the conditions under which they adopt programs or methods that should not have been adopted.

The problem of effective use of microcomputers in schools is a variation on the problem of fostering change in organizations. Computers represent a means for presenting science in an attractive mode with broad appeal that can emphasize abstractions, scientific reasoning, and experimentation. Computers can also be used as "intelligent tutors" to make instruction more effective. Extensive practical use of computers would, however, require very different classroom organization, new teaching materials, easily available and usable software, and different teacher skills in managing different social interaction. It is not enough to focus just on training teachers, or on developing software, or on changing learning groups. All these factors must be related. Interdisciplinary research is needed to exploit findings on how schools can produce better learning through educational systems that might be quite different--and more effective--than familiar ones.

Information and Evaluation of Alternatives

Efforts to develop new curriculum material or instructional systems are by themselves not sufficient to have powerful positive effects on the extent and quality of mathematics and science instruction. Another necessary but not sufficient condition for improvement is that schools be informed about alternatives. Evaluation and dissemination of educational materials and practices should be supported in the areas of mathematics, science, and technology. Interdisciplinary collaboration drawing upon the knowledge and expertise of mathematicians, physicists, chemists, biologists, and social scientists as well as mathematics and science educators will be needed to evaluate existing educational materials in science and mathematics from both a scientific and pedagogical perspective. The reviews and evaluations should include curriculum materials and instructional alternatives developed with the support of NSF and other public and private funding agencies, textbooks and ancillary materials prepared by publishing houses, and materials produced by state departments of education or local public and private schools. Tests of student achievement should also be examined, particularly those used to make judgments about statewide or nationwide performance in mathematics and science.

In addition to evaluation of materials, exemplary and innovative educational practices should be evaluated, including new ways of using computers, use of specialist and resource teachers, and preservice and inservice education. Evaluation results should be given careful scrutiny by scientific and pedagogic experts and then widely disseminated to schools districts, teachers, principals, and other concerned with educational improvement.

3
Experience With Interdisciplinary Research

THE CURRICULUM PROJECTS OF THE 1960s

Scope

In the 15 years between 1959 and 1974, the National Science Foundation invested more than $1.5 billion in science education; the budget increased from $61.3 million in 1959 to $134.5 million in the peak year of 1968 and then declined to $78.5 million in 1974. By far the largest fraction of the funds went to support training activities for individuals--fellowships and traineeships for graduate students in the sciences and institutes for secondary school teachers, the latter representing 50 percent or more of the annual investment during the late 1950s and early 1960s. While the training programs and institutes were traditional in form (i.e., conducted in university settings and largely by university departments and faculty), a third program, the course content improvement program, represented a new social invention (see Philip Handler quoting Harvey Brooks, National Science Foundation, 1975).

Although the curriculum improvement program never exceeded $20 million per year in size and generally represented around 10 percent of the total NSF science education budget, it was responsible for the development of nationally recognized reform curricula in mathematics and science for all levels of precollege education. The characteristics of these curricula, their effects on students, and their impact on education are still being analyzed today. In this chapter, we do not attempt to recapitulate and assess the reform curricula themselves but consider two aspects of the projects supported in the course content improvement program: their ability to attract outstanding scientists to work on precollege science and mathematics education and the extent of interdisciplinary collaboration.

The curriculum development project of the 1960s was perhaps inspired in part by the Manhattan Project. The leading figure in the first of the projects supported by the National Science Foundation was Jerrold Zacharias, who had also been one of the principals in the Manhattan Project. His concept of a curriculum project made possible the participation of talent drawn from far beyond the university or any other single institution. The generally prestigious setting encouraged researchers eminent in their own scientific disciplines to lead and become actively involved in developing precollege science curricula. The principal work structure, summer writing conferences and workshops, brought together individuals from different specialties to create new learning materials. All the projects were characterized by active collaboration among university researchers, college faculty, and school teachers from a particular discipline. At later stages, artists, film makers, designers, and professional writers and editors were also involved.

While the initial high school projects generally did not cross disciplinary boundaries, this focus changed as course content improvement projects for junior high school and elementary school were undertaken. For example, the Elementary School Science Study involved cognitive scientists, physicists, biologists, chemists, mathematicians, engineers, a philosopher of science, and educational researchers, as well as the mix of institutional affiliations and professions represented in the high school projects. Individuals from scientific disciplines who worked in such a project shared its philosophical and pedagogical approach but tended to develop particular units of curriculum strands grounded in their own discipline, rather than developing interdisciplinary curricula. Interestingly, the model for all the curriculum projects, the Physical Science Study Committee--started by Zacharias in 1956, before Sputnik--tried to develop a 2-year physical science course to replace the traditional chemistry-physics sequence in senior high school, but gave up the attempt in favor of reforming just the physics course.

Another type of collaboration emerged as the testing of the new curricula in classrooms began to provide a laboratory for educational research: Lee Cronbach (then at the University of Illinois) worked with several of the projects to design appropriate evaluation strategies; Myron Atkin (then also at the University of Illinois) became interested in research on schools through his work in curriculum development; Joseph Schwab (School of Education, University of Chicago), Fletcher Watson (School of Education, Harvard), and Gilbert Finlay (School of Education, University of Illinois) were drawn into the enterprise as codevelopers and later as evaluators of the whole reform effort. The School Mathematics Study Group (SMSG) conducted a major national longitudinal study of mathematical abilities in an attempt to "turn mathematics education into an experimental science," in the words of E.G. Begle, SMSG's director. This 5-year study (1962-1967) brought together mathematicians, psychometricians, and educational researchers and provided the training ground for many of the most prominent researchers in mathematics education today.

A somewhat different approach to interdisciplinary work was taken by Robert Karplus, who became as recognized for his knowledge and application of Bruner's and Piaget's work in cognitive science as he was for physics research. The science curriculum for grades 1-6 that emerged under his leadership (really two separate programs, one in physical science, one in life science) incorporated Karplus's understanding of cognitive development as well as basic scientific concepts.

Later curriculum studies were explicitly set up to bring together individuals from the behavioral and social sciences with individuals from the natural sciences. For example, Harvard Project Physics (later called Project Physics Course) not only emphasized a broader conception of the subject, including its historical and societal context, but also involved researchers from the social and behavioral sciences in instructional design and evaluation. As another example, the Individualized Science Instructional System, started in 1972, had on its advisory board psychologists, an anthropologist, an economist, a sociologist, a political scientist, and educational researchers as well as chemists, physicists, life scientists, an oceanographer, and an engineer. The objective was to develop minicourses for grades 10-12 that could be put together flexibly either into multidisciplinary courses or biological or physical science programs, all with considerable emphasis on social implications. Perhaps because of the ambitious goals, or because of the timing (after the post-Sputnik reform effort had lost impetus), or because of the attempt to develop multidisciplinary curricula through units that tried to balance theoretical and applied science, or because there was no explicit slot for them in the high school science course sequence, project materials did not enjoy the widespread use in schools that earlier, more discipline-based curricula had experienced.

In the decade since the decline of NSF's course content improvement program, the evidence on the quality and effects of reform curricula has been sifted and assessed numerous times. Some critics have contended that the secondary school materials are mismatched to the competencies of students and teachers (e.g., Arons, 1981). Others found the projects were successful in producing text and laboratory materials of high quality from which many students learned more and better than from the materials that they replaced (e.g., Shymansky et al., 1983). Particularly at the elementary level, however, implementation issues--the training of teachers and the maintenance of kits and materials for hands-on experiments--were not successfully addressed.

What can one learn from the experience of the curriculum projects of the 1950s and 1960s about interdisciplinary research and development? What motivated outstanding scholars to work on these projects? What incentives were provided? What disincentives were there? How was participation in a curriculum project viewed by the participant's institution, peers, professional community? How did views differ depending on one's discipline and type on institution (research university, college, school)? What helped or hindered participants from different university departments, from precollege institutions, from a variety of professional associations, and from private industry in working together effectively?

The committee asked a dozen or so of the key participants in the projects to comment on these questions and also on their perceptions as to whether and how conditions are different today; see Appendix for letter of inquiry. Some of the views of the respondents are presented below.

Context

The national mood, consensus on the need for educational reform, and the wartime experience of successful problem-solving by large teams of scientists provided the foundation for the curriculum development work.

The National Mood

The mood was one of "can-do." Robert Davis:

> This was the time of the Peace Corps, of the beginning of the moon-landing space effort, etc. Great things were seen to be possible. One spoke of "New Frontiers." A new and more optimistic role was seen for the federal government. . . . People really believed that better education and a better society were achievable, provided we made the right decisions and did the right things.

John Truxal:

> In the 1960s, outstanding scholars worked on curriculum projects partly because of the leadership provided by Jerry Zacharias and the MIT group, but more because of the national climate. In 1965, for example, when space and military funding was still easy to obtain, several of us began a switch from space efforts to work with New York's newly elected mayor, John Lindsay, as we tried to apply our backgrounds to urban problems. Today, there seems to me to be no comparable social and ethical forces on the 40-year-old engineer becoming bored with more and more abstract theory in his/her field.

Consensus on the Need

John Mayor notes that "quite a number of scholars worked on the projects because of their recognition of the critical need for improvement of science education." And Glenn Seaborg:

> First, there was a perception of a national problem, a serious deterioration in the quality of education, including in chemistry. Second, at least in the case of chemistry, the whole profession was behind the reform effort. The American Chemical Society had studied the problem through a specially convened committee which urged action to reform the curriculum.

The World War II Experience

Robert Davis:

> I have always believed that the true start of the revision movement was World War II and the Manhattan Project--physicists, previously in the habit of working alone, with relatively inexpensive equipment, discovered that a very large number of physicists could work together in a determined effort to achieve a quick solution to an urgent "practical" problem, while commanding large resources. This entailed a change of self-concept, and after the end of World War II this approach was focussed on other goals. The extreme inadequacy of U.S. education made it an obvious and appropriate target.

Management and Resources

NSF used a direct management style that emphasized the recruitment of outstanding people for the curriculum improvement projects and the expectation that high-quality curricula would be produced. The internal management of the projects was similarly result oriented. Adequate financial support was provided by NSF over the life of a project to ensure orderly progress of the work. Glenn Seaborg:

> Harry Kelly of NSF recruited very able individuals from all around the country, and between ACS [American Chemical Society] and NSF urging, _no one_ who was asked to work on CHEM Study turned down the opportunity. Money was not an issue--whatever was needed was made available. . . . There was a consensus on what needed to be done; there was leadership and good management both in Washington and in the individual projects; and there was willingness to support the effort financially and managerially. . . . Today's situation appears considerably different. Although the quality of education may be of equally great concern, there is not as broad involvement, and those people who are motivated to work on precollege education must compete for scarce funds.

And John Truxal:

> Certainly the concept of the long-term NSF commitment encouraged personal commitments and allowed cautious, step-by-step course development. I have the impression (perhaps untrue) that the Foundation took a more active role in defining a project and encouraging involvement of key people. . . .

Robert Davis makes similar points:

> NSF . . . expected reasonable problem definitions to emerge, and they expected genuine progress to be made. . . . [NSF] made judgments based on the actual work being done . . . NOT solely on proposals and on written reports. This can be an important difference--the best R&D people are not necessarily the most persuasive report writers. . . . NSF [was willing] to accept proposals in a form determined by the proposer, instead of requiring the proposer to conform to some predetermined form that might not be appropriate in a given case.

Jerrold Zacharias:

> Effective research in education cannot be done on the cheap. A system that runs at an annual expenditure of some two hundred billion dollars per year cannot be repaired for anything but a reasonable percentage of that amount. So before you tackle the problems of incentive, collaboration, or institutional pride, you must know where funding stands--the available pattern, its management, its robustness and the soundness or frailty of planning for committed expenditures.

Involvement of Outstanding Scholars

The general climate and the management and resources available for the work helped draw outstanding individuals to the enterprise; their presence helped draw others. Once these people were involved, the intellectual challenge kept many at the task of curriculum reform for a long period. Some prestigious universities also recognized the work as important, although others did not. With some exceptions, only fully tenured faculty could afford the risk of spending time on educational improvement rather than on research in their discipline.

Motivation for Involvement

Henry Pollak:

> [There were] two phases to the involvement: (a) coming to the first summer workshop to try writing curriculum materials, and (b) coming back and persisting in the effort. Undoubtedly, the initial involvement was sparked by money, but then people recognized the tremendous intellectual challenge in the work of taking a piece of mathematics and teaching it effectively to precollege students while keeping the mathematics honest. This turned out to be as tough as research in mathematics per se. . . . The unexpected, exciting intellectual content of the curriculum work kept top-notch mathematicians engaged in it summer after summer.

John Mayor:

> Those projects which were associated with a prestigious professional organization . . . or with a prestigious university . . . had through their association an additional incentive. Adequate financial compensation for six or eight weeks summer assignment in a pleasant environment such as Palo Alto or Boulder was an incentive for some.

Robert Davis:

> From every perspective, the NSF-supported curriculum work was clearly a quality operation. The people at NSF were good; the other participants in PSSC [Physical Science Study Committee], ESS [Elementary Science Study], etc., were good; at every level <u>good sense prevailed, and could be expected to prevail</u>. Who would NOT want to work with Jerrold Zacharias, Philip Morrison, Francis Friedman, Robert Karplus, Andrew Gleason, and Frederick Mosteller?

How Involvement Was Viewed

Henry Pollak:

> There were two types of participants from the research community: full professors who were established in their positions (i.e., senior faculty) and a sprinkling of mathematicians from industry. Nontenured faculty could not take the risk of straying from their research if they hoped to get promoted. As far as the view of peers was concerned, the attitude was: "If you don't tell me [that you are involved in non-research activities], I won't hold it against you." The situation may be somewhat improved now; there are institutions of higher education that give recognition to junior faculty for activities other than research, e.g., the quality of their teaching, their involvement in faculty and campus affairs, contributions to precollege education. However, it probably remains true that attitudes have not changed at the top 100 or so research universities. . . . The problem of getting outstanding scientists and mathematicians involved in precollege education certainly hasn't been solved yet.

John Mayor remembers that institutions generally favored participation, research institutions sometimes excepted. However, he assumes that "the attitudes are a bit less favorable now than 20 years ago, perhaps just because it is being 'done again' and not everyone is sure that it [bringing curricula up to date] was sufficiently successful the first time."

Glenn Seaborg stood in a special position:

> As chancellor of Berkeley, I could ensure that productive young researchers like Pimentel were able to continue their research while working on curriculum projects. Usually, this was accomplished through temporary reduction or elimination of their teaching loads. Working on curriculum projects was recognized as a professional contribution, at least for CHEM Study, and careers did not suffer; in fact, many careers were enhanced by the national visibility of the work. Today, creative researchers would receive less credit for getting involved in precollege education and taking time away from their research and university teaching.

Gerald Holton:

> At least at Harvard, our participation in the Project Physics Course during the whole long period of initial development and testing (1964-1970) was viewed favorably by the relevant administrators as well as by my colleagues in the physics department. In good part this may have stemmed from the long history of involvement of the university, and of physicists in particular, in innovative educational work. . . . In this respect, I believe the attitudes here have remained positive.

Amount and Nature of Collaborative Work

From the beginning, teachers as well as university faculty were involved in the work, though perception of the teachers' role appears to vary among respondents. The original high school projects were focused on a single discipline; later projects often brought together scholars from several disciplines. For the most part, educational researchers and administrators were not involved.

Henry Pollak:

> Essentially, there was no collaborative work involving other disciplines as far as the high school courses were concerned. For each of these, like physics, the emphasis was on reforming the instructional content and teacher training according to the views of individuals from within the specific discipline, e.g., physicists. Also, learning psychology was not very advanced, at least regarding the teaching of mathematics; decisions on pedogogic strategies had to rely on the judgments of experienced teachers. This second factor has changed over the last two decades; cognitive scientists as well as experienced teachers have something to contribute to current reform efforts. . . . Collaboration was present in the 1960s in the efforts to create integrated science/mathematics curricula for the elementary level, notably USMES (Unified Science and Mathematics for Elementary Schools). These collaborations were successful as far as the curriculum materials went; the reason these materials made little headway in the

schools is that the needed effort to train 1.2 million elementary school teachers in how to use the materials was never undertaken.

Pollak also discusses the roles of participants from different types of institutions:

> In School Mathematics Study Group projects, there was a very important collaborative effort between mathematicians, teachers, and educators. Working closely together for two months (in the summer study sessions) meant that a degree of communication and understanding developed between university and school people on what was to be taught and how it was to be taught that did not exist before and has not existed since. Two-day meetings, conferences, etc. don't accomplish this objective, since it takes at least a week before people stop proclaiming their own agendas and listen to someone else.

Glenn Seaborg:

> No collaborative work with people from other disciplines was involved, because the top priority was to reform the high-school chemistry course. However, from the beginning teachers were full partners in the project; their role was critical in keeping the university chemists in touch with the reality of the classroom and ensuring that the materials were teachable. Also, chemistry faculty from smaller colleges--institutions that concentrate on teaching rather than research--were involved, especially in institutes and other teacher training activities. The collaboration of individuals from these three types of institutions--schools, colleges, universities--was key to the success of CHEM Study, and similar collaboration will be needed today.

Arthur Livermore:

> One of the strong points of the Chemical Bond Approach (CBA) project was that we involved high school chemistry teachers right from the start. A weak point was that we didn't listen to them as much as we should have. . . . I don't think any attempt to improve science education will be successful if the recipients of the "improvement" aren't involved

in the action. . . . We didn't involve people in disciplines other than chemistry in developing the CBA materials. We did give some thought to programmed instruction, but we didn't have any learning psychologists discuss this with us. I think we could have benefited from advice by psychologists. Today, of course, there is the added frontier of the use of computers in instruction and in interfacing in the laboratory.

Gerald Holton:

The Project Physics Course products may have been one of the chief models of "collaborative work," involving from the beginning scientists, educators on school and college levels, educational researchers, editors, historians of science, philosophers of science, graphic artists, filmmakers, laboratory equipment designers, reading specialists, etc. The list of significant contributors has 177 names. . . . The three codirectors [consisted of] a physicist and physics historian, a professor in the graduate school of education, and a former high school classroom teacher. I would urge similar arrangements for new curriculum development projects today.

John Truxal:

In the projects with which I am familiar, there was remarkably strong involvement of teachers and educators. I personally believe strongly this involvement is essential--just as biomedical engineering has failed miserably when no physicians are involved. New developments must gain acceptance in a remarkably homeostatic field, so must be very carefully matched to the detailed characteristics of the profession. On the other hand, there was very little collaboration with educational researchers. . . . Whether such collaboration is important today is a difficult question. Cognitive science and "knowledge engineering" fascinate me, but it is not clear to me that there are yet important inputs for curriculum developers.

John Mayor:

I rate the collaborative work with teachers, and its extent, to have been excellent. This same rating cannot be applied to other disciplines including educational researchers. It was difficult to persuade physicists or biologists to work on mathematics projects or to keep them once they started. Similarly, mathematicians contributed little or nothing to projects in the other sciences. In general, little cross-disciplinary collaboration was perceived as necessary in the 1960s. The climate for collaborative research is surely better now, and in my view, the need much greater.

Summary

Obviously, the context of 25 years ago cannot be recreated. Optimism about the ability to solve the nation's educational problems has diminished, while priorities have shifted to a concern with mathematical and scientific literacy for all, rather than emphasizing primarily preprofessional education. This new priority requires even greater emphasis on collaborative work drawing on several disciplines and professions. Furthermore, current management styles and the funding exigencies characteristic of the relevant federal agencies probably preclude the style of project that produced the reform curricula of the 1960s. Given these factors, adaptations or new social inventions are needed for conducting interdisciplinary research that focus on current priorities; deal with the managerial and fiscal constraints of the 1980s; take advantage of advances in the social and behavioral sciences relevant to improving mathematics, science, and technology education, particularly the work on teaching and learning in these fields; and structure participation of teachers, administrators, and other practitioners in a fashion that will alleviate the difficulties of implementing educational improvements. Of particular concern in this connection is the paucity of courses that represent effective subject-matter preparation for either preservice or in-service teachers--a high priority for multidisciplinary research and development.

EXAMPLES OF INTERDISCIPLINARY RESEARCH IN OTHER FIELDS

The problem of how to involve scientists in interdisciplinary research is not unique to education. Strategies and incentives that have led to success in other fields can be examined for their possible application in education, provided differences in circumstance are clearly kept in mind.

The Manhattan Project is often cited as the classic example of successful collaboration of scientists, mathematicians, engineers, and military professionals, though this collaboration was certainly not without tension. A very important factor in keeping the work going was that all the participants were highly committed to a specific and intensely patriotic goal. The crisis context of World War II is probably impossible to re-create for mathematics and science education today. Other factors that may be more replicable were Robert Oppenheimer's leadership and commitment to using multi-disciplinary rather than parallel teams, his personal involvement in the recruitment of eminent scientists from different disciplines, the guarantee of adequate funding, and minimal constraint on the research process by bureaucratic or military procedures. These same factors also characterized the curriculum projects of the 1960s.

Research involving several scientific and engineering disciplines in cooperative work is the aim of the National Materials Program, created in 1960 with the establishment of interdisciplinary laboratories. By 1969, more than 600 faculty members and 2,400 graduate students were participating in materials research in the 12 laboratories, and several thousand research papers were being produced each year. The original method of funding the laboratories through block grants to universities rather than through grants to individual investigators had the goal of stimulating interdisciplinary administration of funds and delegation of authority to local institutions (Schwartz, 1985). In 1972 the requirements were changed further to ensure that not only each laboratory but also individual projects would involve investigators from more than one discipline. Program elements that have helped promote interdisciplinary activity are joint design and development of facilities by scientists from different disciplines, seminars by invited speakers, and inhouse seminars to help educate scientists about the cooperating fields outside their own disciplines.

Environmental impact assessments, which have been funded by government agencies for several decades, often require the expertise of specialists from the natural sciences, engineering, and social sciences. Some of the assessments have failed to integrate the findings of the specialists involved, but others provide examples of effective interdisciplinary research (Williams et al., 1986; Burdge and Opryszek, 1986). Key factors in effective research include: problem definition through interdisciplinary participation, agreement on a conceptual framework that encompasses the various planned research activities, a decision-making structure promoting integration of work toward the common goal, strong management from a principal investigator with sufficient time for the project, regular means of communication and having offices and laboratories physically close, recognition and rewards from the institution for interdisciplinary activity, and a plan for dissemination of results to a variety of potential user groups.

Technology assessment is a relatively new form of interdisciplinary research often involving social scientists, economists, engineers, natural scientists, systems specialists, and lawyers. Rossini et al. (1981) identified several conditions fostering effective collaboration: flexible boundaries among units so as to promote cross-disciplinary team formation and allow for rewards for interdisciplinary activity, careful bounding of the problem before research begins in order to control the scope of the study, and communication among researchers from different fields and some understanding of the interrelationships of the disciplines involved.

Scientific research in health and medicine is another area that frequently calls for interdisciplinary investigations, including collaboration between physicians and scientists. The National Institute of General Medical Services (NIGMS) provides support for biomedical research training that reflects this orientation toward interdisciplinary research. Training grants are awarded to institutions of higher education for support of predoctoral and postdoctoral trainees in specific areas of research. The goal of the predoctoral program is to "provide trainees broader access to thesis research opportunities across discipline and department lines"; the postdoctoral training program focuses on "advanced and specialized areas of research and opportunities to study clinical problems" (NIGMS Announcement, 1984). Applicant universities must provide a detailed plan for training, criteria for trainee selection, mechanisms for quality control, and evidence of plans for the cooperative involvement of faculty members from several departments. For example, the predoctoral program in genetics involves collaboration of scientists in chemistry, biochemistry, cell biology, population and behavioral aspects of heredity, and developmental biology. For another example, the postdoctoral program for training scientists in trauma and burn research includes trauma surgeons or burn specialists as well as scientists in physiology, biochemistry, immunology, and microbiology. Another postdoctoral program is oriented toward new M.D.s to provide them with experience in the methodology and conduct of clinical research on the effects of drug actions in humans, involving knowledge and techniques in such areas as pharmacology, biochemistry, physiology, and analytical methodology. In fiscal 1985, the predoctoral program supported 840 trainees in about 40 universities at a cost of more than $5 million for stipends alone--a substantial federal commitment to training in interdisciplinary research.

SOME THEORETICAL CONSIDERATIONS

The experience with interdisciplinary research can be interpreted in the more general context of what is known about diversity in social systems. The same basic issues arise in collaborative research that are inherent in social institutions of any complexity: differences among the collaborators, various possibilities for organizing the existing diversity, the influence upon the collaboration of the wider contexts of history and society.

The differences among the various participants are not necessarily a problem, though difference is often construed that way. Rather, diversity among collaborators is a resource for doing the work; it is the group's reason for being. When difference is taken to be a production resource rather than an inhibitor to productivity, diversity within work groups is seen in a new light. If there were no differences, there would be no need for structure, for articulation, for action, for knowledge exchange and transfer. Some of the tensions and trade-offs that are inherent in organizing diverse collaborators are discussed below.

Difference and Distance

Multispecialty collaboration involves differences in perspectives, in authority and prestige, and in group and individual interest among the collaborators. The differences in perspective involve values and intellectual positions: a physicist and a sociologist are likely to have differing priorities and viewpoints deriving from their professional specializations (Homans, 1961; Druckman and Zechmeister, 1973). The perspectives of these university researchers may also differ from the professional perspectives of those outside the university, e.g., curriculum developers, school administrators, and teachers. There may also be differences in perspective that are the result of ethnic, racial, and social-class subcultures to which the various collaborators belong (Campbell and Levine, 1972).

Another kind of distance is difference in authority and prestige (Perrow, 1963; Tuschman, 1977; Hollander, 1980). Some people and organizations may have a wide range of action available to them because of their of authority and prestige, while other parties in the collaboration may have a narrow range of options. Moreover, perceptions of authority and prestige may vary among the participants; for example, a teacher's view of a school administrator's authority may differ from that of a research physicist.

There are also differences of individual and group interests--costs and benefits, for example--among collaborators (Aldrich, 1972). A university's interests (and the career interests of the university faculty member) may differ from those of a textbook publisher and from those of an elementary school teacher. Not only may there be differences in costs and benefits among the various parties, but these interests may be realized at different points during the course of the collaboration.

In a realistic attempt to connect various specialties in joint effort, all these kinds of differences must be taken into account organizationally. The presence of difference and distance does not have to lead to problems, provided the work has been appropriately organized.

Organizing Diversity

What to do with the differences? One response is to make room in any program intended to foster innovation for a few visionaries who persist with their iconoclastic notions in the face of organizational pressures and the accepted consensus. Most efforts, however, will have to resolve the problem of coordination among different people, specializations, and institutions (Childe, 1971; Aldrich and Herkes, 1977; Aldrich, 1979). The problem consists of the trade-off between "too much" and "too little": When coordination attempts to produce uniformity among the specialties, the organization can lose its capacity to do complex, interdigitated tasks; when coordination is inadequate, the work of the various parts is not articulated, and the capacity of the organization to do complex work is inhibited. In either case, the work suffers. Coordination is costly in terms of time and money, and, unfortunately, the most flexible kinds of coordination may be the most costly.

The matter is complicated further in that the costs and benefits to the diverse parties in a collaboration may be realized in different ways and at different times during the course of collaboration. Consequently, it is especially important that all parties try to be as clear as possible about the nature and limits of the task on which they are collaborating. This necessity for clarity does not mean that the task may not undergo redefinition as the work proceeds, but only that all the collaborators be party to and understand the changes. Though clarity in itself may not be a sufficient condition for successful collaboration, judging on the basis of the examples described above it appears to be a necessary one.

A quite different option for dealing with the trade-offs between specialization and coordination is to use parallel organization to accomplish the overall aims of the work (Mulford and Rogers, 1982). In some cases, parallel organizations working in tandem can avoid some of the monetary and nonmonetary costs that would come from coordinating an integrated task force. This option is often used in development involving design of a number of complex elements: coordination takes place at the overall planning level rather than among individual task forces. Under such circumstances, however, successful integration requires fairly tight specification of each task and an attendant loss of flexibility. In the past, educational development has been characterized by parallel organization with the frequent consequence that various innovations have not been well adapted to the organizations for which they were designed or even to each other.

Another trade-off involves the advantages and disadvantages of differences in relative status and authority among the collaborators. In the case of collaboration between scientists and the school personnel, differences in status are certainly present; some people claim, in fact, that elementary school teaching is a stigmatized occupation. Persons of higher rank (in this instance, scientists) may be reluctant to enter into collaboration with those of lower rank (in this instance, teachers, school administrators, and curriculum developers) because they fear loss of prestige. Perhaps more important, they also may fear loss of opportunity to enhance their career status and level of prestige--a very real opportunity cost for academic researchers at the beginning and middle of their careers. At the same time, persons of lower rank may be reluctant to enter into collaboration with those of higher rank because they are intimidated by them.

Once a joint effort has begun, anxiety over the potential and actual risks involved may be expressed through outward agreement with the aims of collaboration accompanied by covert resistance, particularly by lower-status participants. For example, change in the methods and content of instruction may be resisted by teachers, principals, students, and parents at the level of a local school district, a school, and a classroom. This sort of resistance may provide part of the explanation for the seeming anomaly of the schools being at once open to change and closed to it (Giroux, 1983). Considerable research on school organizations and on organizational change efforts within them (Berman and McLaughlin, 1974-1975) suggests that teachers may resist passively, but they do resist, particularly when initiatives for change come from the central administration of the school district (Weick, 1976). In such attempts at change, school principals are often caught in the middle.

In their reluctance to change, teachers may be behaving quite sensibly since, at least in the short run, the perceived risks of innovation may outweigh the perceived benefits. Such perceptions of the immediately real versus possible long-term benefits must be taken account of in attempts to stimulate change. If changes in science education are seen by teachers, principals, and parents as both educationally justifiable and not impossibly costly in terms of increased demands on the teachers' already severely limited time and energy, then collaboration to bring about changes might be successful despite the differences in rank and interest among the various participants.

WHAT HAS BEEN LEARNED

The success of past efforts at multispecialty collaboration in the United States, such as the Manhattan Project, may be accounted for by the combination of high legitimacy of aims and perceived professional and financial rewards. It seems unlikely that economic investment in educational research and development will be committed at the scale and with the focus that characterized military research and development during World War II. Nor does the same consensus on aims exist in education. Indeed, given the nature of the public school system of the United States, consensus on aims may be difficult to achieve beyond the global generalities that characterize education in all the states (Goodlad, 1984). These conditions must be taken into account in plans to improve science, mathematics, and technology education, but they do not make interdisciplinary research impossible.

Interdisciplinary research has definite advantages over single-discipline research in addressing complex problems in public policy. The product is more likely to represent different approaches to an issue and be accepted by the audiences and practitioners that are expected to implement it. It also has great difficulties (Sharp, 1983). From reviewing the curriculum development projects, other examples of interdisciplinary research, and the more general experience with diversity in organizations, it is possible to identify several lessons about the development and organization of interdisciplinary research that are applicable to science and mathematics education today. Two recent collections of studies on interdisciplinary research (Chubin et al., 1986; Epton et al., 1983) support these lessons.

Leadership

The principal investigator has been called the key individual in interdisciplinary research. Not only should the person chosen as team leader be committed to an interdisciplinary approach and appreciate the perspectives of different disciplines (Saxberg and Newell, 1983), but he or she must have the capacity to coordinate the work of the other members of the team. The leader also needs to be a strong manager who has sufficient time to commit to the project.

Participation of Disciplinary Scientists

Eminent disciplinary scientists can be recruited to participate in interdisciplinary research that has a specific practical or applied goal. Incentives for recruitment include expectations of funding for the term of the project and a consensus on the importance of the project to the nation or the scientific community. It is also important that all of the team members be favorably disposed toward doing interdisciplinary work.

Role of Sponsors

High-quality interdisciplinary research requires, first, few bureaucratic regulations and requirements and avoidance of unnecessary government oversight. However, a specific requirement that research projects have principal investigators from two or more fields may help ensure multidisciplinary research teams. Alternatively, the incentive of potential funding for research on specific problems may induce universities to form multidisciplinary research teams in response (Handscombe, 1983).

A second critical aspect of fostering interdisciplinary research is the funding agency's mechanism for reviewing proposals. Care must be exercised to draw reviewers from a wide enough spectrum of expertise so that the proposed activities can be judged from the several perspectives to be represented in the work. Since interdisciplinary work, by definition, trangresses the bounds of traditional organization, the review process must, while retaining its rigor, also encompass nontraditional mixes of expertise appropiately matched to the sponsor's goals and program characteristics. The need for care applies not only to the review of proposals: judgment of work in progress as well as of completed projects also requires selection of reviewers who understand the complexities and special requirements of interdisciplinary work.

Third, funding agencies must recognize that interdisciplinary research generally requires more time and money, especially in the early stages of a project, than research within a single discipline (Epton et al., 1983). Three mechanisms available to federal agencies that can provide some stability for interdisciplinary teams are block grants that allow local institutions to administer and manage funds, the establishment of interdisciplinary centers, and the funding of multiyear projects. However, each of them robs the sponsoring agency of some control and flexibility in the disbursement of its funds.

Institutional Settings

Characteristics of institutional structure and management can facilitate or discourage interdisciplinary research. Institutional settings for interdisciplinary research can be characterized along two dimensions: size of research team (large or small) and nature of the institution (university/academic, other nonprofit, for profit, interinstitutional). Depending upon the scope and purpose of the research, there are advantages and disadvantages with each type of setting. Recently, much of the government-sponsored interdisciplinary research in universities has been carried out in "organized research units," which are usually fairly large, semi-autonomous branches of universities that have a specific mission (Epton et al., 1983); the educational research centers funded by the Department of Education are examples of such units. The regional laboratories (also funded by the Department of Education) that assist school systems with the application of research and improvement of educational practice are examples of free-standing nonprofit organizations.

No matter what the institutional arrangement, the host institution needs to create flexible boundaries between units to facilitate the participation of disciplinary scientists. Moreover, institutional recognition and rewards should apply to interdisciplinary research as well as to discipline-based research. The current academic reward system based on peer review tends to lead toward narrow specialization in the choice and management of research, which continually disadvantages individuals interested in working across boundaries. In that respect, an analogous problem in judging interdisciplinary work arises for a host institution as for a potential sponsor. There are, however, effective peer review systems for interdisciplinary research, for example, for the research conducted for the agricultural extension service (Russell, 1983).

Organization of Research Project and Team

The problems to be addressed through interdisciplinary research should be carefully defined and bounded through participation of the scientists from the relevant disciplines and practitioners from the institutions in which the research is to be applied. A common conceptual framework needs to guide all the research activities. Specific steps in planning projects should be completed through such joint efforts of the participants as designing special research tools or planning the dissemination of results.

The two predominant forms of organization of interdisciplinary teams are project organization and matrix organization. A matrix organization is common to mission-oriented research (Low, 1983), but it can produce stress on participants because of role ambiguity, and the team may have poor integration as a result (Stucki, 1986). One means of improving communications is close proximity of project participants. Explicit mechanisms for team communication and interactions are also important.

Any organization of a research team should provide a decision-making structure that ensures interdisciplinary input and development of common objectives for the project. Understanding of other perspectives and the interrelationship of the disciplines involved is important not only for the leader but for all participants in the project.

4
Research Program Alternatives

The main part of this chapter is an examination of several program options for interdisciplinary research in mathematics and science education, and their strengths and weaknesses, in light of the evidence and analysis presented in Chapter 3. The review of program options preceded by a brief discussion of a few dimensions that must be considered in any program planning process, and it is followed by a few words on the need for long-range planning. Throughout this chapter three groups of scientists and educators are envisioned as participants in the research: (1) natural scientists and mathematicians; (2) social and behavioral scientists, researchers in mathematics and science education, and other education researchers; and (3) school administrators and teachers.

PROGRAM DIMENSIONS

The committee's assessment of existing examples of interdisciplinary research and the needs for interdisciplinary research in science and mathematics education indicate that a sponsoring agency should carefully consider a variety of options for research programs. Different program structures and objectives are likely to lead to different kinds of participation as well as different program outcomes. Three major dimensions of program differences need to be considered in program planning: size and time scale, strategy for involvement, and leadership.

Size and Time Scale of Programs

The resources likely to be available will affect not only the overall scale of the program but also the probable size of individual research projects and grants. For example, successful interdisciplinary research has been conducted in large research centers, each involving many scientists from a single institution as well as scientists and educators or clinicians on a full- or part-time basis from across the country. Successful interdisciplinary research has also been fostered through fellowships awarded to individuals and through small grants supporting only two investigators: see, for example, the joint NSF/NIE program involving cognitive and natural scientists, and the resulting projects (described in National Science Foundation, 1981).

With respect to time scale, short-term and long-term are often, but not necessarily, commensurate with small and large. Thus, a program of modest grants to small teams of investigators can be expected to yield results in basic knowledge or application relatively soon (National Science Foundation, 1981:196-198), as can a large investment in a development project for which the basic research base exists (e.g., the Manhattan Project). But small-scale investments in training can be expected to have long-term pay-off, and the large investment necessary to create and sustain research and development centers obviously represents a long-term strategy, even though short-term as well as long-term results can be expected. Agencies sometimes favor programs of small awards because they are more flexible with respect to budgetary fluctuations than are programs that require large-scale investments over a period of years. Program flexibility, however, can turn into program instability, causing the loss of outstanding investigators.

Strategy for Involvement

One type of strategy for interdisciplinary collaboration is for the agency carefully to define the problems in science and mathematics education that are to be addressed and then request proposals for carrying out the work. A different strategy is for the agency to identify eminent scientists and educators who are interested in pursuing interdisciplinary research in science and mathematics education and then allow them to define the nature of the problem(s), develop a plan for research, and lead the research with agency support. A third strategy is to offer inducements to promising young investigators (e.g., through specially designed research grants or fellowships) to work in interdisciplinary settings. For any given program idea, the agency has to decide on the most appropriate strategy for involving scientists and educators.

Leadership

A sponsoring agency has to determine how the leaders who are essential for interdisciplinary projects will be provided. A sponsoring agency and its officials might take a strong role in generating interest and involvement from the scientific community, as was the case in the curriculum projects of the 1960s. Alternatively, programs might give incentives to universities to organize and manage interdisciplinary research projects, as is done in NSF's Materials Science Program. Another possibility is to ask professional scientific or educational organizations to take the lead in planning and developing interdisciplinary research projects. It should be noted again that assurance of at least some stability in program priorities and funding as well as some autonomy for project leaders will help to attract outstanding scientists and educators to interdisciplinary research.

PROGRAM OPTIONS

Considering these three dimensions of program planning for interdisciplinary research and using the analyses presented in the preceding chapters, the committee has endeavored to relate several program options to the major factors that affect and are affected by interdisciplinary research. In Figure 1, the options are listed in the first column, and the factors identified in the committee's analyses as related to successful interdisciplinary research are displayed horizontally. Each program option is discussed below, together with the factors most strongly associated with it, as indicated by the asterisks in Figure 1.

Program	Favorable Climate	Leadership	Quality Personnel	Management Incentives	Funding Stability	Institutional Support	Coordination/ Communication	Product Orientation
Interdisciplinary Research Centers		*		*	*	*	*	*
Recruitment of Top Scientists/Educators	*	*	*		*			
Campaigns to Increase Awareness	*		*					
Demonstration Schools and Classrooms		*		*	*	*	*	*
Institutional Incentive Grants		*		*	*	*		*
Problem-Specific Grants				*				*
Fellowships and Grants for Scientists and Educators				*				

Figure 1 Program Options and Factors that Advance Interdisciplinary Research

Interdisciplinary Research Centers

A large-scale program option for a sponsoring agency is support of one or a few interdisciplinary research centers. This model has been used to encourage research institutions to plan and organize interdisciplinary research programs. According to a recent study by the U.S. General Accounting Office (1986), scientists who are in research centers are involved in more cross-disciplinary research than colleagues who are in regular academic departments.

Research centers can be planned by the sponsoring agency to address specific problems, as is the case for the centers recently funded by the Department of Education, or interdisciplinary research centers can be organized to give institutions flexibility in defining research problems and planning interdisciplinary research. For example, the NSF-supported Materials Research Laboratories and new Engineering Research Centers are funded through block grants in order to encourage universities and research institutions to organize programs of research involving several disciplines. If a center is large, it can also be asked to address systemically related problems in order to counteract the proven ineffectiveness of dealing with any educational problem in isolation.

The conditions that are likely to be positively affected by the creation of research centers are shown in Figure 1. First, the possibility of an interdisciplinary center could stimulate research universities to provide leadership for interdisciplinary work on science and mathematics education. The examples cited above document that block grants can help develop institutional leadership.

Second, appropriate management incentives for fostering interdisciplinary teams can be specified in agency grant requirements. The requirements can also specify the kinds of disciplines and specialists that are desirable in the projects, such as physical or life scientists, mathematicians, science educators, cognitive scientists, and school administrators or teachers. Grant requirements, however, cannot ensure the caliber of scientists or educators that apply, though grant selection can do so if there are enough applicants. Conversely, inappropriate management strategies can discourage participation by scientists and educators: for instance, a sponsoring agency's methods of soliciting proposals and oversight of projects can act as an incentive or disincentive for interdisciplinary work. The amounts of paperwork, bureaucratic monitoring, and reporting that are required were cited as important factors in the outcomes of previous interdisciplinary projects (see Chapter 3).

Third, the commitment of adequate resources is a major advantage of the research center option. A funded center allows both participants and institutions to count on a sufficient level of support for a multiple-year effort to build and maintain effective teams for carrying out substantial projects. An important factor in previous successful interdisciplinary projects was just such a margin of financial support so that the host institution could attract outstanding individuals, develop collaborative working relations, and carry projects to fruition. An additional dividend is that such centers can provide support for junior faculty until they can build a track record and then obtain funds on their own, thus expanding the field. For example, materials science has largely evolved as a recognized interdisciplinary field through the long support of the Materials Research Laboratories. Institutional support in the form of rewards and recognition for interdisciplinary activity, which has been very important in earlier projects, is also facilitated by stable funding. Institutions are likely to be more willing to provide greater professional rewards for interdisciplinary research in the context of a funded research center. Thus, the research center option can increase the involvement of disciplinary scientists and educators and encourage peer recognition for interdisciplinary work, which in turn can reinforce long-term institutional support.

Fourth, coordination of project components and activities and regular communication among participants from different disciplinary backgrounds are possible in research centers, though not without explicit mechanisms. Research centers can provide the opportunity for proximity in physical location as well as funding for meetings and seminars that increase cross-disciplinary communication. The sharing of equipment (e.g., computers and software) that funding of broad projects often entails also is a significant source of collegiality. A full-time project leader is particularly important for coordination and communication, and a center is likely to have a full-time leader. It is not possible to predict, however, whether a research center will facilitate good communications and coordination between scientists and educators. Crossing institutional barriers is particularly difficult, especially if centers are located on university campuses where school administrators and teachers are not likely to be viewed as having equal status with researchers.

Last, product orientation, for example, getting out research results, developing improved teaching methods, or creating better curricula, may be a positive result of the research center option, particularly if the center has some specific problem-solving missions defined from the outset. A funding agency can have an important role in establishing a product orientation, as with the curriculum projects of the 1960s, but it has to avoid over-management that decreases the flexibility of a center.

What kinds of problems of science and mathematics education could most advantageously be addressed through research centers? Drawing on the needs outlined in Chapter 2, likely areas include:

- research and development on the content of science and mathematics curricula;
- analyses of the role of school and classroom contexts in shaping mathematics and science curricula and instruction;
- development of new testing approaches and methodologies; and
- research on how prospective and practicing teachers develop knowledge and understanding of subject matter and associated improvement of preservice and inservice education.

For each of these areas, centers should be charged with carrying out research, development, and--most important--application in a variety of educational settings. The work should be organized around problems, development of solutions, and the application and implementation of solutions, not around broad-based research questions. As a strategy for encouraging fresh viewpoints, a center might offer temporary appointments for 1 to 3 years. Consideration should also be given to creating some centers based on linkages to the areas of practice, e.g., schools, state agencies, university services, textbook publishers, etc., rather than trying to develop the linkages as a consequences of what is produced.

Recruitment of Top Scientists and Educators

A second large-scale option for a sponsoring agency is a program that concentrates on recruiting eminent disciplinary scientists, education researchers, and practitioners. This kind of model was used by NSF in the curriculum projects of the 1960s (described in Chapter 3). The curriculum projects were initiated jointly by prominent scientists and the NSF staff after after unsatisfactory curricula were identified to be a major problem in mathematics and science education. As the reform movement gained momentum, more top scientists and mathematicians were recruited to participate in curriculum development. The scientists and mathematicians designed the projects, recruited others including outstanding teachers, and led the development process.

Strong leadership by a sponsoring agency is always likely to be an important factor in encouraging eminent scientists and educators to become project leaders. Emphasis needs to be placed on giving leading researchers, scholars, and practitioners a wide degree of flexibility and discretion in order to encourage their participation. Given a fixed amount of program resources, this strategy is likely to result in a smaller number of projects being funded than would be the case for a less proactive grants program, since eminent participants will expect (and can obtain for other activities) appropriate resources to plan and carry out their ideas.

If the strategy is successful, it is likely to improve the climate for interdisciplinary research because of the participation of highly regarded individuals. Resource commitment and institutional support also are likely to be positively affected by recruitment of top scientists and educators. However, other steps are needed to ensure successful interdisciplinary activity in science and mathematics education through this strategy. A potential problem with this model is in gaining a balance in the qualifications and status of scientists and educators, particularly since scientists have not usually had high regard for educators. Problems of communication and coordination among project participants may be further accentuated if the participants from the various disciplines and specialties do not have respect for the expertise or views of others in the interdisciplinary team. This situation can result in domination by one perspective, a criticism sometimes made of the 1960s curriculum projects.

A recruitment strategy might be considered for the following types of activities identified as needs in Chapter 2:

- o development of new theories of instruction in science and mathematics that incorporate recent knowledge about reasoning in these fields;
- o uses of new instructional technologies for improving the organization of schools and classrooms for teaching mathematics or science;
- o development of new testing approaches and methodologies; and
- o change in the content of science and mathematics curricula that takes account of new knowledge and procedures in a discipline, new instructional technologies, and new knowledge about the development of student cognitive skills.

Campaigns to Increase Awareness

A third large-scale program option for a sponsoring agency is to develop a campaign to increase the awareness of scientists and educators of the need for interdisciplinary research. Much attention has been given to such indicators of the inadequate quality of precollege science and mathematics education as declines in course enrollments, achievement test scores, and competent teachers. Many scientists and educators are fully aware of these indicators and have some interest in the associated problems. Not many, however, are aware that the complexity of most of these problems calls for an interdisciplinary approach, nor do they have any reason or incentives for participating in interdisciplinary research. An agency could develop a program to explain the nature of the problems in more detail and outline the contributions that could be made toward developing answers. A variation would be a targeted campaign aimed at scientists and educators previously identified as having a strong interest in science and mathematics education. Such a campaign could involve professional scientific and educational organizations and societies through conferences, publications, and networks. Most important, it could provide support for dissemination and application of successful examples of interdisciplinary research in science and mathematics education. Such demonstrations, and perhaps the publication of some serious histories of successful efforts, are needed to provide evidence of the value of interdisciplinary activity for improving education. The suggested program, through emphasizing the importance and effectiveness of interdisciplinary research, would improve the climate for increased involvement of talented scientists and educators.

Areas likely to benefit most from such a strategy include:

- reformulation of the content of precollege science and mathematics curricula based on new knowledge, concepts, and procedures in the relevant disciplines;
- development of educational software in specific subject areas;
- research on teachers' understanding of the concepts and processes of a discipline and how it is acquired;
- analyses and development of effective methods for teaching reasoning in specific disciplines to students with different aptitudes and characteristics.

Demonstration Schools and Classrooms

A medium-scale program option is support of demonstration schools and classrooms. Existing schools and classrooms could serve as hosts for interdisciplinary research and teaching projects in science and mathematics education. This option could be viewed as having similar objectives and participants as the interdisciplinary research centers but, instead of the university campus, the school would be the host institution and the classroom the locus of the activity.

Although such projects would be oriented toward application--demonstration teaching, ongoing assessment, and local curriculum improvement--they could also generate new theory and models for research. An objective of these projects would be to move research from university campuses to schools and classrooms so as to take advantage of the rich experience base of teachers. In this model, researchers with combined science and education backgrounds might have a role similar to clinicians or research professors in teaching hospitals connected to medical schools. The schools and classrooms, while a source of data for research, would also be a source of ideas and new approaches to research.

This program option is apt to foster several conditions related to effective interdisciplinary research. Leadership and involvement of school administrators and teachers would be more likely than with any of the other options, but successful involvement would require that school administrators and teachers have time away from other responsibilities to participate in the project. The strategy would be particularly useful for interdisciplinary projects centered on understanding education practice in schools and classrooms. As with research centers, the sponsoring agency could specify the expected products of the demonstration, or the grant could be more open-ended, with participants defining goals and outcomes.

Agency support for demonstration schools would need to provide adequate resources for involving scientists and researchers from a cooperating university as well as participants from the school. Interdisciplinary projects in demonstration schools--like the research centers--could be an effective way to develop coordination and communication among participants. The locus of the project in a school could have the advantage of lowering the status and authority barrier between scientists and educators. This kind of project could lead to strong support from cooperating institutions, but it would probably need careful planning and development, in the early stages especially, so that participants would indeed gain recognition for their work and products.

The areas that might benefit most from demonstration schools and classrooms are issues involving learning context, which include:

- o teaching reasoning in specific subject areas;
- o assessing the effects of new technologies on organizational change in schools;
- o studies on the importance of learning contexts for curriculum and instructional methods;
- o developing effective models for learning groups and activity-based instruction; and
- o projects that involve community organizations and institutions in improving student learning.

Institutional Incentive Grants

Institutional grants represent another medium-scale program option for encouraging interdisciplinary research. The specific research problem or topic can be selected by the applying institution or the sponsoring agency. The funding level is considerably more modest than that required to support a research center.

An existing model for this option is the Materials Research Group (MRG) grants recently begun by NSF. Five MRG grants were funded in fiscal 1986, each for about $1.5 million for 3 years. The grants are designed as intermediate projects between individual investigator grants and the Materials Research Laboratories. A goal of the program is to involve new institutions in multidisciplinary materials science research. Each institution must propose a project that involves a number of investigators from different disciplines.

Institutional incentive grants for interdisciplinary research in science and mathematics education would have many of the positive elements of the research centers, but each project would involve less funding commitment by an agency. Like research centers, institutional grants would provide incentives for universities and other institutions to take the lead in developing interdisciplinary teams. They may encourage institutions to provide more rewards and recognition for interdisciplinary activity in education than has been typical in the past. An incentive grants program would provide a sponsoring agency with a means of ensuring that funded projects have interdisciplinary participation and a product orientation that is consistent with the purposes of the agency's programs.

In order to encourage scientists to participate in such a grant program, an agency could identify and publicize its interest in interdisciplinary research problems that have theoretical or application linkages to existing disciplinary research. For example, researchers working on the psychology of motivation might be attracted to working on the problem of declining enrollments in science and mathematics at the high school level. Identifying potential interdisciplinary research problems would involve scientists and educators through linkages to their existing interests and work. This approach might help dispel the belief that researchers are necessarily changing their field of research when they work on educational problems.

Several areas seem promising for institutional incentive grants:

- o educational software for science and mathematics;
- o teacher knowledge and understanding of subject matter and strategies for improving teaching;
- o effective models for activity-based learning groups and laboratory instruction;
- o effects of home and school environments on learning;
- o projects that involve community organizations and institutions in improving student learning.

Problem-Specific Grants

A program option possible even under stringent budget constraints consists of grants awarded jointly to two or more investigators to conduct interdisciplinary research on a specified problem. The projects can be closely coupled to priorities that are set by the agency. There can be several grants related to one problem area--as exemplified by the joint NSF-NIE grants of several years ago to support research on cognitive development and learning--or several different problem areas can be identified for which proposals are invited. An agency could provide for several kinds of grant categories for specific kinds of disciplinary collaborations, for example, in physical or life science and cognitive science, in mathematics and curriculum research, or in laboratory-based instruction in science and developmental psychology.

This program option counts mainly on agency design to develop interdisciplinary research teams. The program is likely to attract interest from researchers who are already working on similar research problems, while adding the dimension of interdisciplinary collaboration. Such an approach may be most fruitful when a clearly defined problem exists that should be addressed through interdisciplinary research. It also may be a way of encouraging researchers to team up with practitioners in investigating and improving current practices in schools or in testing experimental materials or instructional methods. Since each grant would be defined by a problem, quite specific products (research papers, reports on improved practices) could be expected.

Interdisciplinary research conducted under a problem-specific grants program could address several areas:

- the effects of learning contexts on curriculum and instructional methods;
- effective models for learning groups in science laboratories and other activity-based instruction;
- development of educational software for science and mathematics; and
- evaluation of the effects of new instructional technologies on change in mathematics and science education.

Fellowships and Grants for Scientists and Educators

Another small-scale option that can be adjusted to match available resources is a program of small fellowships or grants. Such a program allows young scientists and educators who may have ideas and interests but have not as yet established themselves in specific research in a discipline to become involved in interdisciplinary research. A variant is to offer fellowships to established professionals to acquire the tools of another specialty in order to conduct interdisciplinary research. For example, NSF's program of postdoctoral fellowships in plant biology, run by the Divisions of Molecular Biosciences and Cellular Biosciences, awards 20 2-year fellowships for approximately $25,000 per year to new Ph.D.s from related fields who propose a research project in plant biology. During the period of their fellowship, they are expected to acquire the knowledge and tools necessary to continue interdisciplinary work.

This program option offers incentives for involving a new cohort of scientists and educators in interdisciplinary work. It can be run as a separate program or built into some of the large-scale options, such as the center model. It is a long-range strategy that is flexible and carries low risks. This program option can also be used for grants to established professionals to develop leaders of interdisciplinary research in education. The grants might vary in duration from 1 to 5 years.

This program option offers a wide variety of interdisciplinary research possibilities in science and mathematics education, including:

- new Ph.D.s in scientific fields could do research relating to education, such as development and testing of curriculum and instructional techniques for educating prospective and in-service teachers in specific scientific or mathematical concepts or skills;
- Ph.D.s in psychology could test theory and practice for assessing student learning in science or mathematics;
- established scientists, teachers, social scientists, administrators, education researchers, and curriculum writers could work as part of an interdisciplinary team, receiving grants for 50 to 75 percent of their salary, to work in a variety of organizations, including the interdisciplinary centers, demonstration schools, and institutional projects discussed above.

LONG-RANGE PLANNING

Any particular collection of programs, no matter how well designed initially or funded, needs to be examined periodically. As the experience of the last 30 years demonstrates, reform in mathematics and science education will not be lasting if it is based solely on responses to intermittently perceived crises. The National Science Foundation (1983) stated the following objective for current reform efforts:

> The improvement and support of elementary and secondary school systems throughout America so that, by the year 1995, they will provide all the nation's youth with a level of education in mathematics, science and technology, as measured by achievement scores and participation levels (as well as other non-subjective criteria), that is not only the highest quality attained anywhere in the world but also reflects the particular and peculiar needs of our nation.

To obtain this ambitious objective, education research programs should:

- be serial and systematic;
- have well-defined intermediate goals;
- make effective use of existing facilities and programs;
- be specific in their plans of action;

- o include reasonable time limits;
- o include a verification or assessment scheme; and
- o maintain stability and commitment at least until the intermediate goals have been attained.

In order to develop the appropriate goals and sub-goals, specific plans of action, verification schemes, and needed staying power, an agency needs to design a multitiered procedure that will accumulate a synthesis of specialized expertise, perspectives, priorities, and capabilities. At every stage of design, verification, and review, a wide variety of experts should be involved in formulating objectives and outlines for alternatives. For the improvement of curriculum and instruction, for example, planning and review should bring together experts in the subject matter, cognitive science, teaching and learning research, computer applications, and text-book development; school administrators, teachers, students, faculty from institutions of higher education who teach lower-division courses, and employers from industry; and social scientists familiar with implementation problems, developers, and individuals in the business of working with teachers and schools. Review and redesign should continue as the development of alternatives progresses so as to provide a built-in mechanism for continuing improvement of mathematics, science, and technology through interdisciplinary research.

Appendix

Letter of Inquiry

NATIONAL RESEARCH COUNCIL

COMMISSION ON BEHAVIORAL AND SOCIAL SCIENCES AND EDUCATION

2101 Constitution Avenue Washington, D.C. 20418

MMITTEE ON RESEARCH IN MATHEMATICS, ENCE, AND TECHNOLOGY EDUCATION

(202) 334-3290

April 10, 1985

Dear ____________:

I am seeking your help in a study being undertaken by the National Research Council at the behest of the National Science Foundation. Foundation has asked our Committee on Research in Mathematics, Science, and Technolgoy Education (list of members enclosed) to develop strategies for fostering interdisciplinary research in education. The question is simple: How can outstanding mathematicians, scientists from the natural, behavioral and social sciences, and educational researchers and practitioners be attracted to work collaboratively and productively on problems of mathematics and science education?

It seems to us that the history of the 1960s ought to be an integral part of the renewed efforts of the 1980s to improve mathematics and science education in the schools. Your experience as one of the leaders of curriculum reform is an invaluable resource as the country attempts once more to improve the teaching and learning of mathematics and science. We are asking you and about a dozen others to provide some reflections on the projects with which you were involved, especially regarding the processes for doing collaborative work:

- What motivated outstanding scholars to work on the 1960s curriculum projects? What incentives were provided? What disincentives were there? I the climate different now? If so, what incentives are needed now?

- How was participation in a curriculum project viewed by the participant's institution, peers, professional community? How did this differ depending on one's discipline and type of institution (research university, college, school)? To what extent, if at all, have these attitudes changed?

- How much collaborative work -- with other scientific disciplines, with educational researchers, with teachers and educators -- was involved in the projects with which you are familiar? How much was perceived as necessary? What is your view on the need today for such collaborative research?

April 10, 1985
Page 2

- <u>What were some key factors that facilitated or impeded the crossing of institutional and disciplinary boundaries</u>, i.e., helped or hindered participants from different university departments, from precollege institutions, from a variety of associations, from the private sector in working together effectively?

We appreciate that you are probably very busy and have little time to respond in detail. However, we are not asking for a paper but only that you jot down in a page or two your reflections on these issues and other related ones that come to mind. A stamped, addressed return envelope is enclosed for your convenience. If you prefer, respond over the telephone; Senta Raizen, our study director, would be happy to hear from you or answer any questions you might have. Her telephone number is (202) 334-3290.

In advance, thank you very much for your cooperation and assistance.

Cordially,

James G. March
Chairman

Request for Responses*

Dr. Jerome S. Bruner
George Herbert Mead University Professor
New School for Social Research

Dr. Robert B. Davis
Curriculum Laboratory
University of Illinois/Urbana

Dr. Andrew M. Gleason
Professor of Mathematics
Harvard University

Dr. David Hawkins
Distinguished Professor Emeritus
University of Colorado

Dr. Gerald Holton
Mallinckrodt Professor of Physics, and Professor of History of Science
Harvard University

Dr. Arthur H. Livermore
Consultant
Bethesda, Maryland
(formerly, Director of Education Research, American Association for the Advancement of Science)

Dr. William V. Mayer
President Emeritus
Biological Science Curriculum Study Company

Dr. John Mayor
Assistant Provost for Research
University of Maryland

Dr. John A. Moore
Chairperson, Education Committee
Society for the Study of Evolution
University of California, Riverside

Dr. Philip Morrison
Professor of Physics
Massachusetts Institute of Technology

Dr. George C. Pimentel
Chairman, Department of Chemistry
University of California, Berkeley

Dr. Henry O. Pollak
Assistant Vice President
Bell Communications Research, Inc.

Dr. Glenn T. Seaborg
University Professor of Chemistry
University of Calfiornia

Dr. John G. Truxal
Distinguished Teaching Profesor
State University of New York at Stony Brook

Dr. Jerrold R. Zacharias
Education Development Center, Inc.
Newton, Massachusetts

* Affiliation as of April 1985

References

Aldrich, H. E.
1972 An organization environment perspective on cooperation and conflict between organizations and the Manpower Trinity System. In A. R. Negandhi, ed., Conflict and Power in Complex Organizations. Kent, Ohio: Kent State University Press.
1979 Organizations and Environments. New York: Prentice-Hall.

Aldrich, H. E., and Herkes, D.
1977 Boundary spanning roles and organization structure. Academy of Management Review 2:217-231.

American Association for the Advancement of Science
1984 Equity and Excellence: Compatible Goals. An Assessment of Programs that Facilitate Increased Access and Achievement of Females and Minorities in K-12 Mathematics and Science Education. AAAS publication 84-14. Office of Opportunities and Science. Washington, D.C.: American Association for the Advancement of Science.

Anderson, John R.
1981 Tuning of Search of the Problem Space for Geometry Proofs. Technical Report. Department of Psychology, Carnegie-Mellon University.

Arons, Arnold B.
1981 Whither do we hurry hence? In Melba Phillips, ed., AAPT Pathways. Stony Brook, N.Y.: American Association of Physics Teachers.
1983 Achieving wider scientific literacy. Daedalus 112(Spring):91-122.

Berman, Paul, and McLaughlin, Milbrey W.
1974- 1975 Federal Programs Supporting Educational Change. Eight volumes prepared for the U.S. Department of Health, Education, and Welfare. Santa Monica, Calif.: Rand Corporation

Bidwell, C. E., and Kasarda, J. D.
1975 School district organization and student achievement. American Sociological Review 40:55-70.

Boyer, Ernest L.
1983 High School: A Report on Secondary Education in America. New York: Harper and Row.

Brophy, Jere, and Evertson, C.
1976 Learning From Teaching: A Developmental Perspective. Boston: Allyn and Bacon.

Burdge, Rabel, and Opryszek, Paul
1986 On mixing apples and oranges: the sociologist does impact assessment with biologists and economists. In Daryl E. Chubin, Alan L. Porter, Frederick A. Rossini, and Terry Connelly, eds., Interdisciplinary Analysis and Research: Theory and Practice of Problem-Focused Research and Development: Selected Readings. Mt. Airy, Md.: Lomond Publications, Inc.

Campbell, R., and Levine, D.
1972 Ethnocentrism: Theories of Conflict, Ethnic Attitudes, and Group Behavior. New York: Wiley

Carey, Susan
1985 Are children fundamentally different kinds of thinkers and learners than adults? In Susan F. Chipman, Judith W. Segal, and Robert Glaser, eds., Thinking and Learning Skills: Research and Open Questions. Vol. 2B. Hillsdale, N.J.: Erlbaum.

Carnegie Forum on Education and the Economy
1986 A Nation Prepared: Teachers for the 21st Century. The Report of the Task Force on Teaching as a Profession. Washington, D.C.: Carnegie Forum on Education and the Economy.

Champagne, A. B., and Klopfer, L. E.
1977 A sixty-year perspective on three issues in science education: I. Whose ideas are dominant? II. Representation of women. III. Reflective thinking and problem solving. Science Education 61:431-452.

Champagne, A. B., Klopfer, L. E., and Anderson, J.
1980 Factors influencing learning of classical mechanics. American Journal of Physics 48:1074-1079.

Childe, J.
1971 Organization structure and strategies of control. Administrative Science Quarterly 17:163-177.

Chipman, Susan F., Segal, Judith W., and Glaser, Robert, eds.
1985 Thinking and Learning Skills: Research and Open Questions. Vol. 2B. Hillsdale, N.J.: Erlbaum.

Chipman, Susan F., and Thomas, Veronica G.
1984 The Participation of Women and Minorities in Mathematical, Scientific, and Technical Fields. Paper prepared for the Committee on Research in Mathematics, Science, and Technology Education, Commission on Behavioral and Social Sciences and Education, National Research Council, Washington, D.C.

Chubin, Daryl E., Porter, Alan L., Rossini, Frederick A., Connelly, Terry, eds.
1986 Interdisciplinary Analysis and Research: Theory and Practice of Problem-Focused Research and Development: Selected Readings. Mt. Airy, Md: Lomond Publications, Inc.

Clement, J.
1982 Students' preconceptions in introductory mechanics. American Journal of Physics 50:66-71.

Cohen, Michael D., and March, James G.
1974 Leadership and Ambiguity. New York: McGraw-Hill.

Cole, Michael, and Griffin, Peg
1987 Contextual Factors in Education: Improving Science and Mathematics Education for Minorities and Women. Prepared for the Committee on Research in Mathematics, Science, and Technology Education, Commission on Behavioral and Social Sciences and Education, National Research Council. Madison, Wis.: Wisconsin Center for Education Research.

Collins, Allan M., and Stevens, A. L.
1982 Goals and strategies of inquiry teachers. In R. Glaser, ed., Advances in Instructional Psychology. Vol. 2. Hillsdale, N.J.: Erlbaum.

Committee on Basic Research in the Behavioral and Social Sciences
1987 Ten-Year Outlook on Research Opportunities in the Behavioral and Social Sciences. Final report of the committee, Commission on Behavioral and Social Sciences and Education. Washington, D.C.: National Academy Press.

Committee on Research in Mathematics, Science, and Technology Education
1985 Mathematics, Science, and Technology Education: A Research Agenda. Commission on Behavioral and Social Sciences and Education, National Research Council. Washington, D.C.: National Academy Press.

Crosswhite, F. Joe, Dossey, John A., Swafford, Jane O., McKnight, Curtis C., and Cooney, Thomas J.
1985 Second International Mathematics Study Summary Report for the United States. Champaign, Ill.: Stripes Publishing Company.

Cusick, Philip
1983 Secondary Public Schools in America. Paper prepared for the National Commission on Excellence in Education, Washington, D.C.

Cyert, Richard M., and March, James G.
1963 A Behavioral Theory of the Firm. Englewood Cliffs, N.J.: Prentice-Hall.

DeLoache, J.S., and Brown, A. L.
1979 Looking for Big Bird: studies of memory in very young children. The Quarterly Newsletter of the Laboratory of Comparative Human Cognition 1(4):53-57.

Donaldson, Margaret
1978 Children's Minds. New York: Norton.

Dreeben, Robert
1976 The organizational structure of schools and school systems. Pp. 857-873 in J. J. Loubser et al., eds., Explorations in General Theory in Social Science. Vol. 2. New York: Free Press.

Druckman, D., and Zechmeister, K.
1973 Conflict of interest and value dissensus: propositions in the sociology of conflict. Human Relations 25:449-456.

Eccles-Parsons, J., Adler, T. F., Futterman, R., Goff, S., Kaczala, C., Meece, J. L., and Midgley, C.
1983 Expectancies, values, and academic choice. In J. Spence, ed., Achievement and Academic Motivation. San Francisco: W. H. Freeman and Co.

Epton, S. R., Payne, R. L., and Pearson, A. W., eds.
1983 Managing Interdisciplinary Research. Chichester, Great Britain: John Wiley & Sons.

Estes, W. K., Shiffrin, R. M., Simon, H. A., and Smith, E. E.
1982 The science of cognition. In National Research Council, Outlook for Science and Technology: The Next Five Years. San Francisco: W. H. Freeman and Co.

Fantini, M. D. and Sinclair, R. L.
1985 Linking school and nonschool education: public policy considerations. In M. D. Fantini and R. L. Sinclair, eds., Education in School and Nonschool Settings: Eighty-fourth Yearbook of the National Society for the study of Education, Part 1. Chicago: University of Chicago Press.

Fetters, William B., Quingo, Jeffrey A., Suter, Larry E., and Takar, Ricky T.
1983 Schooling Experiences in Japan and the United States: A Cross-National Comparison of H. S. Seniors. Paper presented at the annual meeting of the American Educational Research Association, Montreal, Canada.

Fisher, Charles W., Berliner, David C., Filby, Nikola N., Marliave, Richard, Cahen, Leonard S., and Dishaw, Marilyn M.
1980 Teaching behaviors, academic learning time, and student achievement: an overview. In Carolyn Denham and Ann Lieberman, eds., Time to Learn. Available from the U.S. Government Printing Office. Washington, D.C.: National Institute of Education.

Fox, L. H.
1977 The effects of sex role socialization on mathematics participation and achievement. In J. Shoemaker, ed., Women and Mathematics: Research Perspectives for Change. NIE Papers in Education and Work No. 8, Education and Work Group, National Institute of Education. Washington, D.C.: U.S. Department of Health, Education, and Welfare.

Frederiksen, Norman O.
1984 The real test bias: influences of testing on teaching and learning. American Psychologist 39(3):193-202.

Gemmill, L. M., Bustoz, J., and Montiel, M.
1982 Factors Influencing Mathematics Participation of Highly Able Mexican-American Adolescents. Paper prepared for the National Science Foundation, Washington, D.C.

Giroux, Henry A.
1983 Theories of reproduction and resistance in the new sociology of education: a critical analysis. _Harvard Educational Review_ 53:257-293.

Glaser, Robert
1981 The future of testing. _American Psychologist_ 36(9):923-936.

Goertz, Margaret E., Ekstrom, Ruth B., and Coley, Richard J.
1984 _The Impact of State Policy on Entrance into the Teaching Profession_. Princeton, N.J.: Educational Testing Service.

Good, T. L., and Marshall, S.
1984 Do students learn more in heterogeneous or homogeneous groups? Pp. 15-38 in P. L. Peterson, L. C. Wilkinson, and M. Hallinan, eds., _The Social Context of Instruction_. London: Academic Press.

Goodlad, John I.
1984 _A Place Called School_. New York: McGraw-Hill.

Greiner, L. E.
1972 Evolution and revolution as organizations grow. _Harvard Business Review_ 50:37-46.

Hallinan, Maureen T., and Sorensen, Aage B.
1984 Instructional Grouping and Mathematics Education. Paper prepared for the Committee on Research in Mathematics, Science, and Technology Education, Commission on Behavioral and Social Sciences and Education, National Research Council, Washington, D.C.

Handscombe, R. D.
1983 University-based technology transfer. In S. R. Epton, R. L. Payne, and A. W. Pearson, eds., _Managing Interdisciplinary Research_. Chichester, Great Britain: John Wiley & Sons.

Hawkins, J., and Sheingold, K.
1983 Programming in the classroom: ideals and reality. Pp. 17-18 in M. Cole, N. Miyake, and D. Newman, eds., _Procedings of the Conference on Joint Problem Solving and Microcomputers_. Washington, D.C.: Office of Naval Research.

Herriott, Scott R., Levinthal, Daniel, and March, James G.
1985 Learning from experience in organizations. American Economic Review 75:298-302.

Holdzkom, David, and Lutz, Pamela B.
1984 Research Within Reach: Science Education. Washington, D.C.: National Institute of Education.

Hollander, E.
1980 Leadership exchange processes. In K. Gergen, M. Greenberg, and R. Willis, eds., Social Exchange: Advances in Theory and Research. New York: The Free Press.

Holmes Group
1986 Tomorrow's Teachers. East Lansing, Mich.: Michigan State University.

Homans, George C.
1961 Social Behavior: Its Elementary Forms. New York: Harcourt, Brace, and World.

Hueftle, Stacey J., Rakow, Steven J., and Welch, Wayne W.
1983 Images of Science: A Summary of Results from the 1981-82 National Assessment in Science. Minneapolis: Minnesota Research and Evaluation Center.

Hunt, E., Front, N., and Lunnenborg, C.
1973 Individual differences in cognition: a new approach to intelligence. In G. H. Bower, ed., The Psychology of Learning and Motivation. Vol. 7. New York: Academic Press.

Istomina, Z. M.
1975 The development of voluntary memory in preschool-age children. Soviet Psychology 13(4):5-64.

Jacobson, Willard, and Doran, Rodney L.
1985 The Second International Science Study: U.S. results. Phi Delta Kappan. 66(6):414-417.

Kimberly, John R., Miles, Robert H., and Associates
1980 The Organizational Life Cycle: Issues in the Creation, Transformation, and Decline of Organizations. San Francisco: Jossey-Bass.

Lampert, Magdalene
1986 Improving Quality in Science and Mathematics Education: What Can Research on Teacher Education Tell Us? Paper presented at 1986 Annual Meeting of the American Educational Research Association. Available from the author, Michigan State University.

Larkin, Jill H., and Reif, F.
1976 Physically important integrals with calculus. American Journal of Physics 44(6):515-518.

Leinhardt, G., and Greeno, J.
1984 The Cognitive Skill of Teaching. Pittsburgh, Pa.: Learning and Research Development Center, University of Pittsburgh

Lund, Leonard and McGuire, E. Patrick
1984 Business' role in precollegiate education: a survey of impacts and attitudes (preliminary report). In National Science Board Commission on Precollege Education in Mathematics, Science and Technology, Educating Americans for the 21st Century: Source Materials. CPCE-NSF-04. Washington, D.C.: National Science Foundation.

Low, G. G. E.
1986 Management of scientific staff at the Harwell Laboratory of the UK Atomic Energy Authority. In S. R. Epton, R. L. Payne, and A. W. Pearson, eds., Managing Interdisciplinary Research. Chichester, Great Britain: John Wiley & Sons.

March, James G.
1981 Footnotes to organizational change. Administrative Science Quarterly 26:563-577.

March, James G., and Simon, Herbert A.
1958 Organizations. New York: John Wiley.

McCloskey, M.
1983 Naive theories of motion. In D. Gentner and A. L. Stevens, eds., Mental Models. Hillsdale, N.J.: Erlbaum.

McKnight, Curtis C., Crosswhite, F. Joe, Dossey, John A., Kifer, Edward, Swafford, Jane O., Travers, Kenneth J., and Cooney, Thomas J.
1987 The Underachieving Curriculum: Assessing U.S. School Mathematics from an International Perspective. Champaign, Ill.: Stipes Publishing Company.

Moll, L. C., and Diaz, E.
1982 Bilingual Communications in Classroom Contexts. Final report No. NIE-G-0155. Washington, D.C.: National Institute of Education.

Moyer, Wayne A., and Mayer, William V.
1985 Consumer's Guide to Biology Textbooks. Washington, D.C.: People for the American Way.

Mulford, Charles L., and Rogers, David L.
1982 Definitions and models of coordination. David L. Rogers and David A. Whetten, eds.,

Interorganizational Coordination: Theory, Research, and Implementation. Ames: Iowa State University Press.

Murnane, Richard J.
1985 An economist's look at federal and state educational policies. In John M. Quigley and Daniel L. Rubinfeld, eds., _American Domestic Priorities: An Economic Appraisal_. Berkeley: University of California Press.

National Assessment of Educational Progress
1983a _Reading, Science, and Mathematics Trends: A Closer Look_. Denver, Colo.: Education Commission of the States.
1983b _The Third National Mathematics Assessment: Results, Trends and Issues_. Denver, Colo.: Education Commission of the States.

National Commission for Excellence in Teacher Education
1984 What the Reports Said About Teacher Education: A Summary. Paper prepared for the May 2, 1984, meeting of the Commission. American Association of Colleges for Teacher Education, Washington, D.C.

National Institute of General Medical Sciences
1984 Institutional National Research Service Awards (Announcement). National Institute of Health Guide for Grants and Contracts, Vol. 6, No. 3, Bethesda, Md.

National Science Board
1985 _Science Indicators_. Chapter 6, Education. Washington, D.C.: National Science Foundation.

National Science Board Commission on Precollege Education in Mathematics, Science and Technology
1983 _Educating Americans for the 21st Century_. CPCE-NSF-03. Washington, D.C.: National Science Foundation.

National Science Foundation
1975 _Pre-College Science Curriculum: Activities of the National Science Foundation_. Volume II - Appendix. Washington, D.C.: National Science Foundation.
1981 _Source Book of Projects, Science Education Development and Research_. NSF No. SE81-80. Washington, D.C.: National Science Foundation.

Persell, C.
1977 _Education and Inequality: The Roots and Results of Stratification in America's Schools_. New York: Free Press.

Perrow, C.
1963 Goals and power structures: a historical case study. In Eliot Friedson, ed., The Hospital in Modern Society. New York: The Free Press.

Peterson, P. L., Wilkinson, L. C., Spinelli, F., and Swing, S. R.
1984 Merging the process-product and the socio-linguistic paradigms: research on small-group processes. In P. L. Peterson, L. C. Wilkinson, and M. Hallinan, eds., The Social Context of Instruction. London: Academic Press.

Rakow, Steven J.
1984 Predictors of Science Inquiry Knowledge. Paper presented at the 57th annual meeting of the National Association for Research in Science Teaching, New Orleans, April 30.

Reif, Frederick, and Heller, J. I.
1982 Knowledge structure and problem solving in physics. Educational Psychologist 17:102-127.

Resnick, Lauren B.
1987 Education and Learning to Think. Paper prepared for the Committee on Research in Mathematics, Science, and Technology Education, Commission on Behavioral and Social Sciences and Education, National Research Council, Washington, D.C.

Riley, M. S., Greeno, J. G., and Heller, J. I.
1983 Development of children's problem-solving ability in arithmetic. In H. P. Ginsburg, ed., The Development of Mathematical Thinking. New York: Academic Press.

Rogers, Everett M.
1962 Diffusion of Innovations. New York: Free Press.

Romberg, Thomas A.
1986 Measures of Mathematical Achievement: Problems and Influences. Paper prepared for The National Conference on the Influence of Testing on Mathematics Education, University of California at Los Angeles. Available from the author, University of Wisconsin, Madison.

Rossini, Frederick A., Porter, Alan L., Kelly, P., Chubin, Daryl E.
1986 Interdisciplinary integration within technology assessments. In Daryl E. Chubin, Alan L. Porter, Frederick A. Rossini, and Terry Connelly, eds., Interdisciplinary Analysis and Research: Theory and Practice of Problem-

Focused Research and Development: Selected Readings. Mt. Airy, Md.: Lomond Publications, Inc. (Originally published in *Knowledge: Creation, Diffusion, Utilization* 2(4):503-528, Sage Publications, Inc.)

Rumelhart, D. E., and Norman, D. A.
1981 Analogical processes in learning. In J. R. Anderson, ed., *Cognitive Skills and their Acquisition*. Hillsdale, NJ: Erlbaum.

Russell, M. G.
1983 Peer review in interdisciplinary research: flexibility and responsiveness. In S. R. Epton, R. L. Payne, and A. W. Pearson, eds., *Managing Interdisciplinary Research*. Chichester, Great Britain: John Wiley & Sons.

Saxberg, B. O., and Newell, W. T.
1983 Interdisciplinary research in the university: need for managerial leadership. In S. R. Epton, R. L. Payne, and A. W. Pearson, eds., *Managing Interdisciplinary Research*. Chichester, Great Britain: John Wiley & Sons.

Scannel, D. P., and Guenther, J. E.
1981 The development of an extended program. *Journal of Teacher Education* 32(1):7-12.

Schalock, Del
1979 Research on teacher selection. In David C. Berliner, ed., *Review of Research in Education* 7:364-417. Washington, D.C.: American Educational Research Association.

Schoenfeld, A. H.
1979 Explicit heuristic training as a variable in problem-solving performance. *Journal for Research in Mathematics Education* 10:174-187.

Schwartz, Lyle H.
1985 The Materials Research Laboratories: Their Origin and Impact. Paper presented at the Symposium "Advancing Materials Research" on the 25th Anniversary of the Founding of the Materials Research Laboratories, National Bureau of Standards, Gaithersburg, Md.

Shanker, Albert
1985 AFT's president proposes national exam for teachers akin to tests for professions. *The Chronicle of Higher Education February* 6:19(21).

Sharp, J. M.
1983 A method for peer group appraisal and interpretation of data developed in interdisciplinary

research programs. In S. R. Epton, R. L. Payne, and A. W. Pearson, eds., _Managing Interdisciplinary Research_. Chichester, Great Britain: John Wiley & Sons.

Shymansky, James A., Kyle, William C., Jr., and Alport, Jennifer M.
1983 The effects of new science curricula on student performance. _Journal of Research in Science Teaching_ 20(5):387-404.

Stage, E., Kreinberg, N., Eccles-Parsons, J., and Becker, J.
1985 Increasing the participation and achievement of girls and women in mathematics, science and engineering. In S. S. Klein, ed., _Handbook for Achieving Sex Equality Through Education_. Baltimore, Md.: Johns Hopkins University Press.

Stake, Robert E., and Easley, Jack A., Jr.
1978 _Case Studies in Science Education_. NSF SE-78-74. Available from the U.S. Government Printing Office. Washington, D.C.: National Science Foundation.

Sternberg, R. J.
1977 Component processes in analogical reasoning. _Psychological Review_ 89:353-378.
1984 Toward a triarchic theory of human intelligence. _The Behavioral and Brain Sciences_ 7:269-315.

Stevenson, Harold W., Shin-Ying, Lee, and Stigler, James W.
1986 Mathematics achievement of Chinese, Japanese, and American children. _Science_ 231:693-699.

Stucki, Jacob C.
1986 A goal-oriented and pharmaceutical research and development organization: an eleven year experience. In Daryl E. Chubin, Alan L. Porter, Frederick A. Rossini, and Terry Connelly, eds., _Interdisciplinary Analysis and Research: Theory and Practice in Problem-Focused Research and Development: Selected Readings_. Mt. Airy, Md.: Lomond Publications, Inc.

Summers, Anita A., and Wolfe, Barbara L.
1977 Do schools make a difference? _American Economic Review_ 67(4):639-652.

Task Force on Education for Economic Growth
1983 _Action for Excellence: A Comprehensive Plan to Improve Our Nation's Schools_. Denver, Colo.: Education Commission of the States.

Troost, Kay Michael
1985 Society and science education in contemporary Japan. In Margrete S. Klein and F. James Rutherford, eds., Science Education in Global Perspective: Lessons from Five Countries. Boulder, Colo.: Westview Press, Inc.

Tuschman, M.
1977 A political approach to organization: a review and rationale. Academy of Management Review 2:206-216.

U.S. General Accounting Office
1986 University Funding: Assessing Federal Funding Mechanisms for University Research. GAO/RCED-86-75. Washington, D.C.: U.S. General Accounting Office.

Vobejda, Barbara
1985 Facing teacher competency tests. The Washington Post April 22:A10.

Walberg, Herbert J., Harnisch, Delwyn L., and Tsai, Shiow-Ling
No date Mathematics Productivity in Japan and Illinois. Unpublished paper, University of Illinois at Chicago and Urbana.

Weick, Karl E.
1976 Educational organizations as loosely coupled systems. Administrative Science Quarterly 21:1-19.

Weiss, D. J.
1983 New Horizons in Testing. New York: Academic Press.

Williams, Anne S., Nielsen, G. A., Shovic, H. F., Stuart, D. G., Reuss, J. W.
1986 Impacts of large recreational developments upon semi-primitive environment. In Daryl E. Chubin, Alan L. Porter, Frederick A. Rossini, and Terry Connelly, eds., Interdisciplinary Analysis and Research: Theory and Practice in Problem-Focused Research and Development: Selected Readings. Mt. Airy, Md.: Lomond Publications, Inc.

Woodson, R. L.
1982 Helping the poor help themselves. Policy Review: The New Quarterly Journal of the Heritage Foundation 21:73-86.

Yager, Robert E.
1983 The importance of terminology in teaching K-12 sciences. Journal of Research in Science Teaching 20(6):577-588.

ISBN 0-309-07798-2